THE
GENTLEMAN'S
GUIDE
TO
KAREZZA SEX

Copyright © 2020 Nick Brothermore

www.brothermore.com

This book is not intended as a substitute for professional medical advice. You should regularly consult a health professional, particularly with respect to any symptoms that may require diagnosis or medical attention.

This book is dedicated to my wife,
whose beauty and love inspire me every day.

TABLE OF CONTENTS

FOREWORD
BY LUKE EILERS

As a popular men's advice YouTuber and coach to hundreds of men, I don't exaggerate when I say every man should read this book. This book is electric. Open your mind and be willing to go down the rabbit hole with Nick Brothermore's *The Gentleman's Guide To Karezza Sex.*

This book brings something radically different to the personal development, relationship, and sexuality worlds. Not only will you learn about Karezza sex, but you'll learn how to effectively navigate yourself with women, how to step into your full masculine power, and how to become a leader among men. This book is massively important.

The Gentleman's Guide To Karezza Sex is a book about enlightened sex and sexual transmutation, written for men by a masculine man. His language can at times be explicit, even raunchy. Yet, in our politically correct and sensitive world, Manhattan-based writer and coach Nick Brothermore is refreshingly unafraid to boldly speak what he believes and explore the edge. I see this book spreading like wildfire among top performing men.

Reading this book gave me a strong belief that I can live my dreams. Reading this book gave me a strong belief that I can have an amazing relationship. Reading this book gave me a strong belief that I can have the energy, focus, and genius to achieve my huge goals. Reading this book gave me the strong belief that I can be a powerful man. Reading this book gave me a strong belief in myself, my fellow humans, and in life itself. This book is the roadmap that every man needs.

Years ago, I was addicted to pornography and went to a therapist for my porn addiction. My therapist introduced me to the concept of Karezza sex through the book *Cupid's Poisoned Arrow*. The result was a complete paradigm shift regarding sex. I healed from my porn addiction, stopped jerking off, started directing my sexual energy toward purposeful and higher pursuits, and became a new, much improved man.

As a guy steeped in the personal development world, I thought, "*Why had I never heard about this before? It's almost too good to be true. How have these ideas been underground for so long?*"

Now, for the first time, Nick Brothermore has written a guide to Karezza sex specifically for men. The knowledge and wisdom he bestows in **The Gentleman's Guide To Karezza Sex** is unlike anything you've previously read or heard. This is sex meets personal development. This book fulfills a massive need.

Men are struggling in our modern world. We used to be warriors, builders, farmers, explorers, hunters. Now we stare at screens all day. It's hard to feel like a man in the current era. Depression, anxiety, lack of confidence, and diminished hope are rampant. There are very few admirable masculine role models.

Porn addiction is a hidden epidemic. Some men can barely get a date. When a man does enter a relationship, it is often tumultuous and ends with a traumatic breakup that can take years to recover from. When you look at the lustful, pornified, degenerate sexuality that is the norm in today's world, doesn't it make you suspect that we may not be thinking about sex in the best way?

I believe that **The Gentleman's Guide To Karezza Sex** will emerge as a classic. 10 years from now, many women may refuse to date men who don't know about Karezza sex. The concepts in this book will make you an incredible lover. I know multiple Karezza couples who all report the same amazing benefits. Karezza sex is the future, the next frontier for humanity, the next revolution in human history. This is more important than Elon Musk going to Mars.

A world that practices Karezza sex will bring bountiful healing, love, and harmony to humanity. The discord and angst felt between the sexes today can be healed through these practices and paradigm shifts.

As Brothermore notes, practicing Karezza sex makes you a pioneer. Listen to your body, be your own authority, and continue your research. Coupling sexual transmutation practices with meditation or similar grounding activities should prove beneficial.

The Gentleman's Guide To Karezza Sex will completely change how you think about sex. Some deep in group-think may initially brush off these ideas. This book may ruffle some feathers. While I can't personally vouch for every provocative sentence in this explosive volume, I truly believe this book will supercharge your life in the most beautiful way. Read this book with an open mind and get ready for a life-transforming ride.

Welcome to the next sexual revolution!

-Luke Eilers

YouTube: GoldJacketLuke

www.goldjacketluke.com

CHAPTER 1:
THE HEAVENLY PLEASURES OF KAREZZA SEX

WHO THIS BOOK IS FOR

The Gentleman's Guide To Karezza Sex is for men looking for a straightforward, no-holds-barred, raw discussion of Karezza sex from the male perspective. It will teach you everything you need to get started and be successful. This book is for men who want to take their lives to the next level and are unafraid to deviate from established norms in order to make that happen.

The Gentleman's Guide To Karezza Sex is for free thinkers, true believers, and wild dreamers. It's for entrepreneurs, hustlers, go-getters... and every man who aspires to become one.

The Gentleman's Guide To Karezza Sex is for pioneers, for men who have the balls to be at the forefront of a renegade movement. It's for the bold gentlemen who are ready and willing to go balls deep for extended sessions every night... all for the betterment of themselves, their woman, and humanity.

The Gentleman's Guide To Karezza Sex is for men who are sexually experienced, but it's also for virgins. It's for men who are comfortable with women and also for men who are still finding their way. It's for any man who's interested in turning his sex life into an art form.

The Gentleman's Guide To Karezza Sex is for men who are sick of the letdown feeling after orgasm, tired of ejaculation sapping their energy, and weary of feeling needy and addicted. It's for men who recognize the futility of trying to succeed in life without the necessary focus, energy and direction to do so. This book is for men who want to change all that.

The Gentleman's Guide To Karezza Sex is above all for men who believe in love: the lovers. It's for men who believe that sex is nature's most beautiful act and that men and women are capable of magic in bed that transcends mere lust and biology. This book is for men who believe in the raw power of sexual energy and want to learn how to channel it into greatness. This book is *especially* for those men because it's the playbook for making that happen.

WHO THIS BOOK IS NOT FOR

The Gentleman's Guide To Karezza Sex is not for men who don't want a deep sexual and romantic connection with the right woman. For that is one of the greatest joys available to you during your lifetime. This book is not for men who don't want to grow.

The Gentleman's Guide To Karezza Sex is not for men who lack an adventurous spirit. It's not for men who don't yearn to break away from the pack. This book is not for men who only want no-strings sex without a raw and honest connection. It's not for men who aren't willing to be vulnerable and real in bed.

The Gentleman's Guide To Karezza Sex is not for men who believe they already have everything 100% figured out. Because no matter how much you already know, this book is so jam-packed with powerful, straightforward techniques, strategies, and solutions that something in these pages will absolutely blow your mind and give you a new perspective.

The Gentleman's Guide To Karezza Sex is not for men who don't want to be their best, don't want a better relationship, and don't want greater success. Because that's what this book will deliver to men who read it mindfully and put it into practice. The best part is you'll achieve all this with just one simple habit, repeated near-daily. Sound too good to be true? It's not.

A STRAIGHTFORWARD PROMISE

For every ninety-nine life improvement hacks that fail to deliver, there's that one unexpected gem that comes out of nowhere and changes your life. Could Karezza sex be that life hack for you? Could *The Gentleman's Guide To Karezza Sex* be the book that changes your life permanently? I promise you it will be.

If you read this book with an open mind and work consistently to apply the simple Karezza sex habit, a new world will open up to you beyond what you ever dreamed possible. A world of peace, a world of beauty, a world of focus, love, productivity, health, happiness, abundance... and the most exquisite pleasure.

The purest definition of Karezza sex is connected, loving, mindful, controlled, gentle, respectful sex without orgasm or pursuit of orgasm. This book carries forth in that spirit. This book is as true as it gets to real Karezza sex in the real world as practiced by a real man who has utilized these techniques to achieve great happiness, success, and fulfillment. The Karezza sex in this book is raw, real, uncomplicated, and as straightforward as it gets.

TRIGGER WARNING

This book contains frank sexual language and depictions. This is an explicit how-to book about the nuts and bolts of Karezza sex written for real men. You can handle it. If you find yourself getting aroused by the straightforward discussion of Karezza sex in these pages... good. Use it as motivation to go out there, find a woman, treat her right, and try this out for yourself.

A BRIEF HISTORY OF KAREZZA SEX

Karezza sex is revolutionary. It's the single most powerful habit a man can add to his daily routine. And yet Karezza sex is not well known or understood by the masses. It's certainly not a topic of polite conversation. Karezza sex is never taught in sex education. Nor is Karezza sex mentioned in official publications aimed at educating the public about every conceivable manner of sex except the only one that actually empowers a man to rise above his lesser self and claim his place among the heroes and greats.

But that's the way it's always been. You see, Karezza sex - or more generally non-orgasmic, non-ejaculatory sex - is nothing new. Quite the opposite, the concept dates back thousands of years and probably much further. Considering the powerful benefits of the practice, and weighing that against the discipline Karezza sex requires, it stands to reason that throughout history a small, select group has tapped into this transformative power while the vast majority have sadly jizzed their potential away.

The golden age of non-ejaculatory sex was during the Han and Tang Dynasties (206 BC–907 AD). Chinese Taoists tapped into the power of semen retention and non-ejaculatory intercourse as a spiritual practice. They called their unconventional method *The Joining of the Essences* and sex was understood as the comingling of male and female energy, which enhanced the Jing (life force) and Qi (vitality) of both participants. These early Taoists correctly viewed sex as vital to our spiritual elevation. However, the rise of Confucianism during the Middle Ages buried most of this wisdom deep underground, where it would remain for many centuries.

In the 1800s, American spiritualists and health reformers once again advanced the idea of "male continence" as a path to health and success. In 1896, physician Alice B. Stockham published the landmark book *Karezza, Ethics of Marriage*, proposing non-orgasmic sex among both men and women for the betterment of health and relationships. Stockham, a free-thinker and pioneer, coined the term Karezza, borrowed from the Italian for "loving touch."

In 1931, J. William Lloyd published *The Karezza Method, or Magnetation: The Art of Connubial Love* which built on Stockham's earlier work and offered a male perspective.

In 1937, Napoleon Hill published his landmark *Think and Grow Rich*. With 20 million copies sold, this book brought the concept of sexual transmutation out of the shadows and into the mainstream - with a uniquely 20th century American slant. Hill documented the power of sexual transmutation as a key to unlock wealth, success, and happiness. Over the last century, Hill's prescription for sexual transmutation has gained considerable steam as a personal development practice among men.

In 2009, Marnia Robinson's exhaustively researched treatise *Cupid's Poisoned Arrow* revived interest in Karezza sex for the 21st century, injecting neuroscience into the discussion and offering male readers a valuable female perspective on sex without orgasm. Since then, Karezza sex has become a topic for popular sex blogs and YouTube videos, but it hasn't yet fully broken into mainstream awareness. Which brings us to the present.

While not widely practiced, awareness of Karezza sex is approaching a modern-era high. Growing numbers of men have jettisoned pornography and masturbation from their lives. Eventually, most of these men get into relationships with women. But if they practice orgasm-sex, their energy is sapped. On the other hand, men who *avoid* sex and relationships altogether statistically have more health problems, shorter lives, and less success.

This conundrum leaves many men looking for a middle ground. Or better yet a holy grail: sex as a fountain of energy, harmony, love, and happiness. This yearning has led to a growing interest among men in Karezza sex as the ultimate personal development super-hack.

EJACULATION VS. ORGASM (THE REAL MEANING OF RETENTION)

Taoists refer to *semen retention* as the key to enlightened sex. In their view, loss of semen (not the accompanying orgasm) depletes a man's energy and traps him on a lower spiritual plane. Of course, this begs the question, is it possible to have orgasm without ejaculation. Indeed, it is. There is even an offshoot practice called Sexual Kung Fu which trains men to *dry orgasm* - either not ejaculating at all or reverse-ejaculating back into the body. While this may be a worthwhile practice for some men, it largely ignores another likely scenario: that refraining from orgasm itself is the REAL key to enlightened and empowering sex.

Scientifically, much research remains to be performed on these matters. But on a common sense level, it's quite easy to understand why training oneself to abstain from the most powerful 'drug' ever known to man (sexual orgasm) would reap great rewards. Indeed, the anecdotal evidence continues to roll in, and it's overwhelming: men who refrain from orgasm (either solo or in a relationship) report great benefits in all aspects of their lives: confidence, vitality, focus, drive, success, attraction, creativity, peace of mind, relationships, and more. In *The Gentleman's Guide To Karezza Sex* the term "orgasm retention" encompasses *both* retaining your seed (no ejaculation) and retaining your energy (no orgasm).

11

KAREZZA SEX VS. TANTRIC SEX

If you're interested in Karezza sex you've likely also encountered the term Tantric sex. The two are similar in many ways. Tantric sex originated from Hinduism nearly 5000 years ago. Like Karezza sex, Tantra emphasizes sex as a spiritual practice and is more focused on the journey than the destination. Both Karezza and Tantra are strongly rooted in the concept of sexual transmutation - that sex energy is a sacred force to be cultivated and channeled to a multitude of higher purposes.

The major difference between Tantric sex and Karezza sex is that most forms of Tantra involve orgasm. Many popular Westernized forms of Tantric sex even tout *multiple orgasms* and *full-body orgasms* as a selling point. Karezza sex, on the other hand, involves maintaining arousal and heavenly pleasure for long stretches but without the need for orgasmic release to feel the act is perfect and complete.

THE BENEFITS OF KAREZZA SEX

Before embarking on your Karezza sex journey, let's run through the benefits you can anticipate accruing along the way. Consistent Karezza sex will change your life dramatically. The benefits can be broken down into four parts: the benefits of sex, the benefits of a strong and lasting romantic relationship, the benefits of orgasm retention, and the benefits of sexual energy transmutation.

THE BENEFITS OF SEX

Sex is therapeutic. In fact, sex is scientifically proven to benefit us physically, mentally, emotionally, and socially. Human touch, intimacy, trust, vulnerability, triumph: sex fuses powerful elixirs together unlike any other cure.

Sex is a super-activity that strengthens and heals from every angle. But capitalizing on these benefits depends on utilizing sex properly. Sexual impulses run amok have the power to destroy. When we treat sex with the respect and honor it deserves, it can make us nearly invincible.

Studies show that sex fortifies the immune system, increases energy, cures insomnia, boosts confidence, reduces the risk of heart attack and stroke, lowers blood pressure, and strengthens one's sense of well-being. Science also indicates the more sex you have, the more benefits you accrue. That's great news for Karezza enthusiasts, who typically enjoy much more frequent sex and lengthier sessions than orgasm-sex couples.

THE BENEFITS OF A STRONG AND LASTING ROMANTIC RELATIONSHIP

According to research, people in loving long-term romantic relationships are happier, healthier, more successful, and live longer. As a highly social species with advanced pair-bonding capabilities, humans possess a built-in capacity for deep, romantic love that left unmet leaves us feeling less than fulfilled. This sense of lack hampers our mood, performance, and success. A healthy long term relationship may be one of the master keys to a thriving life, but a relationship will only benefit you if it's stable and loving.

With its emphasis on deep, loving connection, Karezza sex magnifies the benefits of a traditional relationship. Communication, loyalty, synchronicity, and caring are all enhanced by Karezza sex. The relationship dynamic is that of a never-ending honeymoon - light years better than what most couples in standard relationships settle for.

THE BENEFITS OF ORGASM RETENTION

The benefits of orgasm retention begin to accrue immediately after you decide to abstain. Much of the initial benefit is mental: a sense of hope, a sense of direction, a magnetic certainty you are on a fruitful path. After ten days or so we start to look better, sound better, focus better. A sense of peace and calm gradually permeates. After twenty days, many men describe a feeling of "I can handle anything" beginning to saturate their awareness.

The early Taoists, of course, knew this. They recognized that sexual depletion saps one's life energy. It leaves you empty and dull. The majority of men orgasm 5...10...15...20+ (you know who you are) times per week. These poor souls squander their entire lives in recharge mode, never getting to that 2-3 week period where significant benefits begin to kick in, let alone to the greater benefits that come with longer retention streaks. Karezza gentlemen, on the other hand, are always fully charged, full of life force, and ready to take on the world with confidence and determination.

Another benefit of orgasm retention comes from training oneself in the practice of delayed gratification. Modern life is a war on your brain's ability to put off short term pleasure in favor of long term gain. The more often short term pleasure is pursued, the harder the impulse becomes to resist. This is because the brain's prefrontal cortex, which houses our delayed gratification ability, becomes atrophied. But without a strong prefrontal cortex, great success is nearly impossible. ADHD is one common manifestation of an atrophied prefrontal cortex. Other common manifestations include obesity and addiction.

Fortunately, like any muscle, the prefrontal cortex can be trained and built into something magnificent and powerful. Orgasm retention is the most efficient way to train and strengthen your delayed gratification muscle because you are resisting the world's strongest drug - orgasm. Karezza sex gives you all the benefits of orgasm retention plus the benefits of sex and a loving relationship. Not a bad deal.

THE BENEFITS OF SEXUAL ENERGY TRANSMUTATION

Sexual energy is the most raw and base of all energies. Because sex energy is so raw, it is malleable. Transmutation means changing one substance into another. Sexual transmutation means channeling and changing sex energy into other forms of energy.

We transmute energy instinctively all the time. Trying to avoid thinking about sex? Get creative and productive. The more charged up you become, the more creative and productive you must become to channel your attention away from the possibility of orgasmic release. That's where genius kicks in. Man will go to great lengths to distract himself from sex when he adopts such a discipline. What he achieves in the process is usually the foundation of his greatness.

KAREZZA SEX IN TODAY'S WORLD

Something's changed in today's world. We're feeling the effects everywhere. Something's not quite right. Something's worse. Many people have accepted the idea that societal decline is just the way it goes - but when has that ever been the case before?

One large contributor to societal rot is rampant daily use of pornography. Once a dirty little secret, porn is now promoted as natural, healthy, and mainstream. Why? Some say it's a symptom of widespread moral decay. Others call it a conspiracy to subjugate the masses into passive and helpless sheep. Still others believe it's an inevitable byproduct of technological advancement. Whatever the root cause, anyone who's experienced the negative effects of porn use can tell you they are dire.

In today's pornified world, Karezza sex is the ultimate countercultural act. Practicing Karezza sex is a statement - to yourself, to your lover, and to the world: *I reject orgasm, I reject instant gratification, I reject an average life, I reject using my partner as a sex doll while I fantasize about depravity, I reject the inhumanity of it all, the foolishness of it all, the pointlessness of it all. I want to rise above. I am determined to be better. Even if no one else wants to or has the ability, I DO AND I WILL.*

TWO TYPES OF MEN

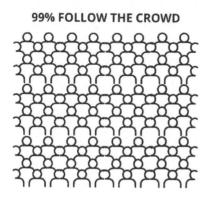

99% FOLLOW THE CROWD

**1%
CHART THEIR
OWN COURSE**

Karezza sex in today's world is a full-frontal assault on society's hollow values, its pornified heroes, and its empty assurance that "it's all good." Karezza sex in today's world is the embodiment of the belief that things can get better, that there is hope, and that what we do every day matters. Karezza sex in today's world is an anomaly: a sex positive practice that treats the body as a temple, one's partner as a treasure, and sex as a meditation on love, beauty, and life. Karezza sex in today's world can be a restorative force to turn our energy and values around toward something more organic and sustainable.

Karezza sex in today's world is revolutionary. This book will give you a solid foundation to start practicing Karezza sex, get your woman on board, and transmute your sexual energy into greatness. Welcome to the revolution!

CHAPTER 2:
A COMPLETE COURSE IN KAREZZA SEX

WHAT KAREZZA SEX IS

Karezza comes from the Italian *carezza* (loving touch). The *zz* is pronounced *ts* like *pizza*. The simplest definition of Karezza sex is sex without orgasm or the pursuit of orgasm. But there's a little more to it than that.

Karezza sex is journey-based as opposed to destination-based sex. Karezza sex is rejuvenation, a spiritual practice[1], energy awareness, and the ultimate manifestation of the mind-body-spirit-sex connection. This chapter will give you concrete guidelines on what to aim for (and what to steer away from) as you embark on your Karezza sex adventures. Later chapters will dive further into advanced techniques and strategy.

---

[1] Spiritual practice in this context refers to enhancing one's spirit or energy. Karezza sex is not a religious practice and you don't need to be religious or brazenly spiritual to enjoy the benefits of Karezza sex.

WHAT KAREZZA SEX IS NOT

Karezza sex is not fucking, it's not banging, it's not screwing. Karezza sex can be very passionate and energetic but it's not violent, it's not out-of-control, it's never disrespectful. Karezza sex is not porn sex. It's not painful, it's not humiliating, it's not ugly. It's not the type of sex 99% of people are having these days.

Karezza sex is not the type of sex that drains you afterward. Karezza sex is not about "getting off" but about getting on (and staying on) until you're both fully satisfied, energized, recharged and at peace, even if it takes an hour or two.

Karezza sex is not quick. When quickies do occur out of necessity or tight schedule they are usually followed ASAP with a longer session. The magnetic pull between Karezza lovers becomes so strong, you'll both want to spend a lot of time in bed - deeply connected.

SETTING THE SCENE FOR KAREZZA SEX

Karezza sex is an extension of your relationship. The better the relationship, the better the sex will be. In turn, better Karezza sex further improves your relationship. It's a positive feedback loop. To get the most out of Karezza sex, you must step up and be the man in your relationship. Show your woman you value, love, and respect her.

Carry yourself like a wise, strong, patient leader. How? Become one - it's the only way. This is important because a woman will only follow you down this path away from conventional sex if you emanate the message that you are worth following. Of course, your body can convey that message in bed, but leadership is a 24/7 business.

Be kind, be paternalistic, be on your purpose. Be a good, loving, gentle leader in and out of bed. Compliment her often - sincerely. Notice what she does right. Thank her for the little things women do for men that we take for granted. Tell her how beautiful she is. Women deserve to hear this regularly. Make her feel good about herself in specific areas where you know she needs confidence. Build her up. Make her feel happy and good. What transpires when your clothes come off will be an extension of all this.

In a harmonious relationship, Karezza sex becomes a cherished nightly ritual where you and your partner lay bare your entire beings for each other's heavenly bliss. It's a beautiful experience, so whatever you can do to improve the quality of your relationship - do it. It will pay off a million times over in the bedroom.

THE POWER OF TOUCH

Touching should be done so often in your relationship that it's second nature. Touching your partner communicates powerful messages: *I love you, we're connected, you're mine.* It also keeps the sexual fires stoked. Women are very sensual creatures with erogenous zones all over their bodies. This makes them naturally attuned to touch energy.

You can touch your woman almost anywhere very innocently and effectuate an exchange of sexual energy. Practiced regularly, habitual loving touch makes it incredibly natural and easy to initiate Karezza sex when nature calls. In fact, it becomes almost automatic.

KISSING IS KEY

You can't have Karezza sex without kissing. Technically, you could. But what would be the point? A kiss communicates: *You are loved, I want to taste you, I want your germs, Let's become one,* and so much more. Kissing should be part of your daily relationship routine. Steal a kiss when she's least expecting it. Women love that. Kiss her in public. Women love that even more. Those little *I love you* kisses you give her at home? Give them to her in public every now and then. Every woman loves to be kissed with other people watching. It makes her feel special. It makes her feel sexy.

When it comes time to initiate Karezza sex, kissing is a great way to transmit your level of desire and escalate. Kiss her passionately and deeply. Invent a new language with each other that can only be communicated in sweet kisses. You might be surprised how easy and fun this can be. Put your creativity to the test.

Karezza sex is "no-rush" sex. Taking your time during the kissing stage (clothes-on or clothes-off) can be a very rewarding and intimate experience in itself. Run your fingers through her hair. Kiss her lovingly. Make her forget all her problems. Make her wet and eager to open herself up to your energy.

KAREZZA FOREPLAY

When it comes to foreplay, there are various opinions as to what's "Karezza" and what's not. On one hand, you have those who maintain Karezza foreplay should be limited to kissing, gentle touch, breathing exercises, loving affirmations, and other modest techniques.

On the other hand, there are those who insist Karezza foreplay should be anything-goes so long as nobody orgasms. This second group might embrace pussy eating, blowjobs, 69, fingering, stroking... and more.

For reasons we'll discuss, most Karezza enthusiasts find a gentle, comfortable groove somewhere in the middle. In this section, we'll cover a wide range of foreplay options, not to give the impression that they're all essential, but because this is a comprehensive guide. At its core, Karezza sex is primarily about intercourse, but you've got to start somewhere.

Foreplay sets the tone for your sexual encounter - ideally a long, very pleasurable one. Foreplay is an energetic middle ground between kissing and full sex. Foreplay done right is about honoring the escalation, taking time to savor the anticipation, and meditating together on what's about to happen. Foreplay done right is about getting warmed up but not overheated. It's about stoking each other's energy until there's nothing left to do but put it in.

AWAKENING POLARITIES

The awakening of sexual polarities during foreplay is extremely pleasurable to both sexes. Women feel at one with their vagina, its softness, its malleability, its resilience, its mystery, its sweetness, its beauty, its magnetic pull, its status as the most highly prized and sought after thing on earth. Women delight in taking on

23

the identity of the vagina - the willing and eager co-conspirator in the great and essential ritual about to be performed.

For men, sexual polarity occurs when you feel at one with your penis. Everything about you that's good and noble is channeled into your cock. You become a vessel for the archetypal masculine energy that exists in our universe. Strong, dominant, rigid, energetic, hopeful, adventurous, bold, loving, playful, and proud.

The difference between Karezza foreplay and regular foreplay is that Karezza foreplay builds toward a mindful and controlled exchange of energy vs. an animalistic and out-of-control one. Make it a point to establish this gentle intent from the start - it will greatly improve the quality of your entire interaction. When stimulating each other's genitals, for example, do it in a more slow, loving, meditative way.

FINGERING

Is it possible to finger your woman lovingly as opposed to lustily? Absolutely. Perhaps you've done so already. Karezza fingering is not what goes on in porn. Karezza fingering is not forceful or violent. It doesn't involve making nasty faces or saying despicable things to each other. Karezza fingering is the opposite of that.

Karezza fingering is a chance to give your woman a slow, sensual, mindful warmup. It's a loving manual exploration of - and engagement with - your woman's vagina. Meditate on polarity, connectedness, and the cradle of life as you lovingly finger her pussy.

24

Pro Tip: Steer away from the clitoris and towards the labia and vulva (see diagram below) to give her a more loving and less lusty warm-up.

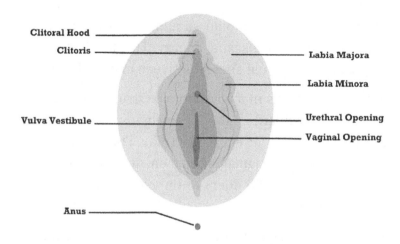

STROKING

Many times while you're making out and gently fingering your woman, she'll be inspired to stroke your cock as well. Like Karezza fingering, Karezza stroking should be slow, loving, and connected - your woman's meditation on your manhood and the fact that it will be inside her soon.

Women have a very special connection to the penis. It's the magic wand that activates their full energetic potential. Just as pussy saves a man from the stagnation of separateness, penis saves women. Meditate on your power, your strength, your leadership, and your love for her as she gently caresses your manhood.

WARNING: ACTIVE ENERGY VS. PASSIVE ENERGY

One important thing to note regarding Karezza foreplay is the difference between active (yang/masculine) sexual energy and. passive (yin/feminine) sexual energy. During Karezza sex, a man should be mainly in touch with his yang/active sexual energy. This facilitates flow and transfer of sexual energy between man and woman.

Putting your penis in a passive role (stroked, sucked, or passively ridden) too much can cultivate yin/passive/feminine energy in a man. This is one reason masturbation is so damaging to men - it turns your penis from the subject (the doer) to the object (the done-to). This feminizes you.

That's not to suggest you must avoid these positions outright. But be aware and mindful of the dynamics at play. One solution is to double down on your active, penetrating mindset when engaging briefly in such passive pleasures.

ORAL SEX

Karezza foreplay can also involve oral sex. However, you may find yourself naturally deemphasizing oral as it's a lower form of energetic exchange - far less efficient than penis-in-vagina.

As a foreplay technique for awakening polarities, oral sex can be effective so long as both partners stay in the right mindset and don't slip into an animalistic orgasm-centric mentality. This is difficult, but for those who can do it, oral sex has the potential to be a sweet, gentle, loving piece of a successful Karezza sex encounter.

CUNNILINGUS

Is it possible to eat pussy with love instead of lust, as a form of spiritual meditation? Indeed. You can orally engage with vagina in a loving and connected way. How? First, forget about technique. Second, forget everything you've seen in porn.

Karezza cunnilingus can be a beautiful way to charge your woman's polarity and put you both in touch with her feminine essence. Clitoral stimulation should not be the main focus as it will steer your woman toward orgasm. Think of Karezza cunnilingus as making out with her pussy. Slow, loving, tender. Get lost in the gateway to life.

FELLATIO

Karezza fellatio should be less of a blowjob and more like slow, meditative penis worship. Karezza fellatio should not be mechanical, or sloppy, or strenuous. Many women overdo it on blowjobs because it's what they or past boyfriends have seen in porn and adopted as normal sexual practice. But there's nothing sexy about your girl gagging up spit, eyes watering, face turning red as you choke her with your cock.

Karezza fellatio is about your woman giving you gentle kisses, loving licks, and perhaps a long, slow suck or two. But be careful. Overstimulation of the head during Karezza foreplay can put you in an orgasm mindset, so don't be afraid to politely request she slow down or back off a bit. Since this is the opposite of what most guys ask for during oral (*"less stimulation and more spiritual connection please"*), this request may indeed make her melt.

69

69 has fascinated men probably since the dawn of time, and for good reason. What's not to like about having your cock sucked while simultaneously indulging in the pleasures of eating pussy. It seems very natural and right. Loving, respectful Karezza 69 is possible but you'll want to keep a few pointers in mind.

First, make sure your woman is on board. Many women love 69 but there's a sizable number who are self-conscious about having their ass in your face. If your girl falls into that camp, try circling back around to 69 once you've established successful Karezza sex for a few months. Once she's experienced a profound new level of intimacy and connection with you, her self-consciousness will likely melt away. Once your woman is on board, keep it gentle, loving, and focused on awakening polarities.

The next thing to remember is don't get too visual. This one's easier said than done because there's just something about *that view.* It's hard not to become animalistic and triggered toward orgasm by the sight, smell and taste of a woman's hindquarters in your face. Newbies should be careful here. Close your eyes? Do it in the dark? Finding solutions can be a lot of fun.

SEX TOYS AS FOREPLAY

Karezza sex is a pure and controlled exchange of sexual energy between two human beings. Anything that creates a layer of separation tends to lessen that energy. Most things people do with sex toys you can also do with your body in a more connected and mindful, less mechanical way.

Avoiding sex toys brings you and your partner into closer contact with each other and reinforces that sex is best as a back-to-nature experience.

PORN AS FOREPLAY

We've probably all seen enough pornography to last a lifetime. If you haven't, good for you. You've avoided one of this world's most insidious traps. Thinking about using porn to get warmed up for Karezza sex? Skip it. Watching strangers fuck on screen won't lead to a connected, fulfilling sexual exchange because your subconscious doesn't understand who you're having sex with - your partner or the women onscreen.

Couples who say they use porn in a positive way actually sacrifice true intimacy for lesser thrills. Porn is an efficient way to generate orgasmic frenzy, but a poor way to cultivate the authentic sexual energy required for Karezza sex.

KAREZZA INTERCOURSE

Now you're ready for the main event. Karezza sex is primarily penis in vagina sex. Why make this distinction? Because Karezza sex requires flow of sexual energy. That energy flows most purely and efficiently through our genitals as opposed to other body parts. Plus, what man doesn't enjoy the sensation of his penis inside a vagina?

In a successful Karezza relationship, you'll get about as much of this as you can handle.

Karezza intercourse is often slower than traditional sex. This slower pace comes about naturally as you mindfully explore the pleasurable nuances of the male/female connection.

Karezza intercourse normally lasts much longer than typical orgasm-sex. Karezza couples also have sex much more frequently than other couples. Karezza intercourse gives both partners a true sense of becoming one. Yin and Yang together as an energetic whole - one in body, mind, heart and spirit.

Karezza intercourse amplifies our essential Jing life force and our vital Qi energy to fuel higher pursuits. Since you never feel drained, the energy you create can also be reinvested into more sex with exponential results.

When the journey is the destination, you become an expert sexual navigator. Hours and hours of slow, mindful sex add up. Karezza gentlemen become much more proficient lovers than their orgasmic brethren. You will gain gigolo-like insight and intuition into the lay of the land. You will learn to speak a secret, quiet language only the most elite lovers ever decipher.

Karezza sex is a tool any man can use to become a legendary lover. No nut-buster can compete with what you offer a woman in bed. Your woman will know she has the best and love you deeply for it.

During Karezza intercourse, keep your mind geared toward loving connection, sexual energy, and keeping it within a sustainable zone. Give your woman the full strength and power of your masculine energy. Bathe in the renewal of her feminine energy and vaginal embrace.

With practice, you'll learn to diffuse sexual energy throughout your body and achieve a calm, peaceful polarity, remaining rock hard and connected for long stretches, exchanging sexual energy without entering the orgasm danger zone. This requires mental training and practice, but the result is heaven on earth.

KISSING DURING INTERCOURSE

During orgasm-sex, kissing is sacrificed because as men, we don't get the best view with lips locked. Karezza sex is less visual, more about touch and physical sensation. Forgoing orgasm, you become less fixated on the view. This naturally leads to more making out.

During Karezza sex you will shift in and out of positions, but for the most part you won't want to stop kissing for long. Kissing communicates love and profoundly compliments the penis-in-vagina connection. Kissing amplifies the benefits of Karezza sex and gives us an opportunity to connect on multiple levels simultaneously.

DANCE OF THE SEVEN CHAKRAS

Exchange of sexual energy is a full body endeavor. When two lovers line their bodies up perfectly, something spectacular happens. There's no better way to have Karezza sex than mouth to mouth, body to body, hand to hand, forehead to forehead, chest to chest, belly to belly, dick in pussy. The connection it creates is unsurpassable.

31

Why does full body contact feel so perfect and natural during Karezza sex? The answer lies in our chakras. Hinduism describes seven chakras, or energy centers, in the body. Different body parts house different energies. Those butterflies in your stomach, that lump in your throat, that head-rush of excitement, that boner that won't quit. These are everyday manifestations of the same concept.

THE SEVEN CHAKRAS

7. Crown Chakra (SPIRIT)

6. Third Eye Chakra (INTUITION)

5. Throat Chakra (COMMUNICATION)

4. Heart Chakra (LOVE)

3. Solar Plexus Chakra (CONFIDENCE)

2. Sacral Chakra (CREATIVITY)

1. Root chakra (ENERGY)

When you engage in full body-to-body sex, all seven of your chakras line up completely. Your *root chakras* connect at the genitals. Your *sacral chakras* line up just below the belly button. Your *solar plexus chakras* line up just below the rib cage. Your *heart chakras* line up at the chest. Your *throat chakras* line up at the throat and are activated by kissing. Your *third eye chakras* line up at the forehead. Your *crown chakras* are located at the top of your head and are activated by occasionally stroking each other's heads during intercourse while the other six chakras are aligned.

Once all seven chakras are lined up and connected, magic happens. This occurs during regular sex too, but usually just for a couple minutes before switching to a more visual position to escalate the titillation level. A couple minutes aren't enough to process and absorb the full power of this connection. You'll want to spend a lot of time in this configuration. It's where the real Karezza sex benefits accrue.

For couples with a large height differential, don't worry about exact symmetry of the heart, solar plexus, and sacral chakras. Get the anchor chakras (root, throat, third eye, and crown) in place and the energy force created will naturally pull the middle three into optimal alignment.

Pro Tip: Here's where daily pushups and weight training come in handy. When your arms and upper body are strong you can hover over your woman in a variety of pleasurable configurations while keeping the seven chakras fully engaged. With creativity and enthusiasm, there are a million different variations and ways to connect up close.

DANCE OF SEVEN CHAKRAS

NIPPLE STIMULATION DURING INTERCOURSE

If you love boobs, Karezza sex is for you. Breast and nipple stimulation release the "love hormone" oxytocin, so it's a natural fit for a style of sex based on generating loving energy. Sucking on a woman's nipples is extremely therapeutic - perhaps one of the most rejuvenating practices on earth for a man. Doing it while you're rock hard inside her is pretty much all any man wants out of life. That's an exaggeration, but not by much.

Loving oral or manual nipple stimulation during intercourse feels even better for the woman because her nipples are one of her most erogenous zones. In fact, make sure she lets you know if you're driving her too close to ecstasy. This can happen to a woman through nipple stimulation because it releases love hormones - and women feel sexiest when bathed in love. With practice, tit sucking and fondling can become a very rewarding and valuable aspect of Karezza sex.

THE POWER OF STILLNESS

Karezza sex is sex without orgasm or the pursuit of orgasm. Beyond that, there are principles but not rules. Some say Karezza sex should be slow. Some even say it should be nearly motionless. Others say none of that matters, just follow the energy and let the experience unfold.

The truth is there are many flavors of Karezza sex depending on the personalities, energy, and preferences of the participants. You can have intense, enthusiastic Karezza sex and perform a perfect energetic exchange. Other times a more tender, contemplative vibe might suit the exchange best. And don't forget to explore the power of stillness.

Remaining still, cock parked in vagina is a tremendously powerful experience not to be missed. During orgasm sex, most couples are too self-consciously programmed toward friction and getting off to "stop and smell the roses," to revel in the moment. When you do this, it's as if time freezes.

Remaining motionless inside your woman, you truly feel the penis-vagina connection, your energy flowing into her, and you absorbing hers. You will notice a profound sensation of her vagina enveloping you, embracing you, you'll feel it expand and contract as she breathes. The rhythms of your bodies connect and start to synchronize. This is the spiritual-sexual connection you've always dreamed of.

Even if you're the more energetic type, you owe it to yourself and your partner to incorporate periods of stillness into your Karezza sex routine. They don't have to last long. Start with a minute or two of this connected sexual meditation. If you and your partner enjoy it you can build up to longer durations.

SEX TALK DURING INTERCOURSE

Karezza sex can be verbal or nonverbal, but when starting out it can help to be somewhat verbal. Loving, intimate words will help you both re-program your ideas and feelings about sex and connecting. Changing the narrative around sex and verbalizing these feelings (and higher ones you aspire to) can help you reset the meaning of sex in your relationship.

The key is honest, kind, loving talk. Stay away from nasty porn sex talk and just be real. Tell her how much you love and respect her. Praise her. Tell her everything about her that's beautiful, inside and out. Talk about how much you love this intimacy and connection. Tell her you love becoming one with her and want to keep getting closer and closer. Tell her how therapeutic she is to you, how much being inside her energizes and strengthens you. Let her know you hope she feels the same way.

Tell her that you love watching her opening up and surrendering and enjoying herself, and you love putting a smile on her face. Tell her you love watching her let go and relax and be free. This type of talk, done sincerely and sparingly, gets women extremely wet and receptive to exchange of sexual energy.

This might not sound very sexy on paper, but in the midst of a Karezza connection this stuff will make your woman melt and open herself lovingly to your male sexual energy. A woman needs to feel that it's okay to let down her guard and surrender completely.

EYE CONTACT

The eyes play a different role in Karezza sex. At times your eyes may be closed since you'll be doing a lot of deep kissing. At other times, you can use the power of eye contact to enhance your connection. A tremendous amount of energy and communication is exchanged through eye contact. It's very intimate. During Karezza intercourse, eye contact can work in conjunction with sweet talk to lock in a solid connection.

When you make eye contact with your woman during Karezza sex, you want to communicate things like *I love you. You're beautiful. You're safe. We are one. I am proud to be your man. I am strong. You make me happy. I have unlimited energy, under complete control.* Make her feel your energy. A woman's hormones don't give her access to the same level of dominant energy you have - so she needs to get this safe, dominant energy from you. It's an essential ingredient for a woman to grow and thrive fully.

Her eyes will communicate her vulnerability and willingness to submit. Submission is a beautiful thing. We are all dominant and submissive in different ways. The bedroom is where man establishes order by giving the woman a primal dose of dominant energy. And he gratefully receives her submissive energy. This is not a violent conquering, but a loving agreement between two connected souls that "we are a part of nature and this is the way."

A NOTE ON "DOMINANCE"

It should be noted that "dominance," in the context of sexual energy practice, is just another word for leadership. To dominate is to prevail, to feel powerful, to lead the sexual dance. Exhibiting leadership characteristics in and out of bed makes women feel safe, secure, loved, and comforted. This is not authoritarian leadership. It's gentlemanly, empathetic leadership as a service. Simply put, it's the channeling of pure masculine yang energy.

VISUAL STIMULATION

During orgasm-sex, men typically enjoy positions that give them a bird's eye view of the woman's body and all the action. With Karezza sex, you'll likely break this habit. Once you learn to operate on sensation rather than sight, a deeper world of sexual pleasure opens up. Watching feels cheap compared to *fully experiencing*. Plus, visual positions make orgasm retention more difficult. Of course you can still enjoy brief glances at the transaction in progress, but it definitely won't be your main thing.

Avoiding porn makes the shift away from highly visual sex much easier. When your optic center receives sexual imagery via porn on a regular basis, you'll need visual stimulation in bed too. The problem is, when you zoom out to a visual position, you can't align your seven chakras for full body energetic exchange, which requires deep kissing and bodies touching all the way down to the genital embrace.

CONNECTING FROM BEHIND

Sex from behind can be extremely intimate and connected. There's much to admire about a woman's backside and going in from behind gives you a chance to enter her in a different, more primal way. When going in from behind, there are two distinct approaches: spooning-style positions and doggy style positions. In spooning-style positions, your bodies are in close contact, while in doggy style positions, the bodies mainly interact at the genitals.

Doggy style is high on many men's lists of great orgasm-sex positions. There are few more enticing views on earth than looking down and watching your cock slide in and out of a woman while her ass moves hypnotically in rhythm. Many gentlemen also enjoy lightly spanking or fondling a woman's derrière in this position, and many women like that too. So what's the problem? None really. Doggy style isn't forbidden in Karezza sex. But it probably won't be your go-to position.

Doggy style is visually overstimulating to most men. Simply put, it's much harder not to bust a nut in this position (although harder does not mean impossible).

The much bigger issue with doggy style in Karezza sex is you are not face-to-face. Once you experience the profound intimacy of face-to-face and body-to-body

Karezza sex, doggy style will feel very shabby in comparison.

Spooning-style positions, on the other hand, allow for a closeness and intimacy that doggy style does not. In these positions, the man is behind the woman but their bodies are touching closely. Wrap your arms around your woman and enter her from behind. The profound connection achieved can be extraordinary.

Spooning positions actually have more in common with face-to-face sex than with doggy style - the full body chakra alignment, the kissing, the eye contact. It's also a great position to whisper sweet talk in your woman's ear while you fondle her breasts and penetrate her pussy.

CONNECTING FROM BEHIND

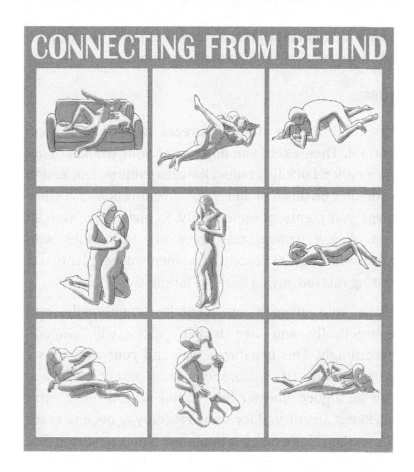

FANTASY

During orgasm-sex, many men resort to mental fantasies to spice things up. Biologically, fertilizing the same partner over and over isn't nearly as thrilling as the porn-fueled fantasies we can concoct in our minds. But fantasizing during sex robs you of a truly connected exchange.

One of the great benefits of Karezza sex is that avoiding orgasm keeps you in the moment and with your woman.

You will stop fantasizing about other scenarios with no effort on your part. It just happens naturally.

LUBE

Extra lubrication during Karezza sex doesn't seem natural. Then again, you don't want your woman to get sore either. Luckily for most Karezza couples, lubrication shouldn't be much of an issue. The entire Karezza ethos gives you plenty of opportunity to make your woman wet. A few women may have physical issues with lubrication, but 99 percent of women will get plenty wet during relaxed, loving Karezza foreplay.

Open your woman up mentally, emotionally, and energetically and her female juices will respond accordingly. This is nature's way and your woman is a part of nature. Of course, spit is also a part of nature and can be a good booster lube if you need a bit of extra slickness on entry. If for some reason you need to reach for artificial lube on a particular occasion, go ahead. But don't use it as a regular shortcut to making her wet.

Pro Tip: Your woman's level of lubrication can be used as a handy gauge to monitor whether you're doing Karezza 'right.' For a full guide to this important topic see *Chapter 6: Jing Juice: Taoist Wet Pussy Secrets.*

THE OTHER HOLE

Karezza sex has no hard and fast rules except don't orgasm. But it does have a definite objective: loving, controlled exchange of sexual energy. Penis-in-vagina sex is by far the best way to achieve this. The closer and more intimate the better. But what about anal? If you keep it loving and focused on polarization and energy exchange, can you have Karezza anal sex?

On one hand, anal seems part of porn culture, something most people don't desire until they start watching porn. On the other hand, a woman's ass is a very intriguing instrument and you can't judge a man for wanting to strike up a tune on it every once in a blue moon. You can't blame a woman for enjoying it either.

Thousands of years ago, the Taoists made positive references to anal sex in their sacred sex guides. These were the inventors of semen retention, you may recall. Yet there are some valid reasons for keeping anal to a bare minimum. The most important is respecting your woman's body. No matter how much porn tries to convince us otherwise, the ass is not a sex organ per se. The unfortunate among us have witnessed closeups of porn stars after engaging in excessive anal - it isn't pretty. So if you do anal, consider keeping it brief, gentle, and infrequent. Remember, your girl will follow your lead and that's a responsibility.

The next thing to keep in mind about anal as it relates to Karezza sex is that a big part of anal's appeal is the thrill of the *verboten* - the rush of putting it where it doesn't belong. This is a very dopamine-based thrill which may tie closely in the brain to pursuit of orgasm for many men. It's probably a good idea to start your Karezza practice without any anal, at least until you become attuned to your authentic sexual energies and discover whether it's something you truly desire or just a kinky thrill you picked up from porn.

Anecdotally, many Karezza enthusiasts report that anal is not part of their routine. "Penis in vagina feels so perfect - why settle for less," they say. Other couples may see anal as the ultimate act of loving dominance and submission.

Despite anal's growing mainstream acceptance, there's a strong argument to be made that it's a rather profound misuse of sexual energy. So close, yet so far away compared to the energetic superiority of the penis in vagina connection.

As for fingering your woman's asshole during from-behind Karezza sex, this can give both you and your woman quite a dopamine rush - the excitement neurochemical. This may feel thrilling, but is likely to trigger the urge for orgasm. With practice, loving ass fingering is likely possible, but be aware it's risky business and a distraction from the energy work in progress.

As an alternative "bonus move" try sucking on and fondling your woman's nipples during face to face intercourse. This will give both you and your woman an oxytocin rush (the bonding/love hormone), enhancing the sexual experience in a sustainable and retention-friendly way.

Whether to incorporate anal into Karezza sex is ultimately between you and your woman. Look deep inside yourselves and decide whether, in the context of your relationship and the encounter, anal sex seems respectful, affirming, constructive, loving, and congruent with your goals and your identity. Use the answer as your guide.

HOW OFTEN TO HAVE KAREZZA SEX

How often you have Karezza sex will vary from couple to couple. The takeaway is that you should make it a priority. See it as part of your personal development routine and track your progress.

As men, our interest in sex is much keener than our interest in other subjects. Sex is the most fascinating thing on earth to most of us. That inclination is famously portrayed as a flaw or a joke in mainstream culture. The truth is, it's not a joke or anything to apologize for. In fact, it will be your greatest superpower once you channel that interest into a successful Karezza sex practice.

In terms of concrete numbers, start out aiming to have Karezza sex more often then you were having orgasm-sex. Build from there. A good number to shoot for is at least 5 times per week. 7 to 10 is even better. Treat Karezza sex just like exercise, nutrition, meditation, or any other part of your daily routine.

With time, you'll naturally find yourself in the "every night club." Be a respectful and loving leader to your woman, apply the techniques in this book, and don't be surprised if she asks for it morning, noon, and night.

HOW LONG KAREZZA SEX SHOULD LAST

The average orgasm-sex encounter lasts 5-10 minutes. Karezza sex takes longer because each session is a form of renewal. The therapy and renewal we experience during Karezza sex takes time. Every day we experience thousands of energetic micro-exchanges - scattering our focus and energy in many different directions. Karezza sex is your daily opportunity to plug in and recharge on every level.

Highly satisfying and renewing Karezza sex usually takes at least 20 to 30 minutes. But due to sheer enjoyment of the act, it's not unusual to find your sessions averaging an hour or more. The more hours you log having Karezza sex, the more your life will improve.

Imagine the huge confidence boost of walking down the street knowing you've had more hours of sex over the last month than any of the other men you see. Lengthy Karezza sessions also improve your skills and sense of energy flow.

Here's a reality check. Hours of intimate Karezza sex won't happen amid arguing, hostility, or indifference. You must keep your relationship in top form. Give her what she needs outside the bedroom in terms of love, listening, closeness, and respect and you'll earn the chance to act it all out in bed as a reward.

At this point you may be wondering if you have the time for so much Karezza sex. If you don't have it, make it. Karezza sex is one of the most profitable investments of your time possible. To make more time, cut out passive and virtual pursuits like entertainment, spectator sports, fandom, video games, news, and social media. You only have so many hours available and Karezza sex will pay dividends unlike anything else you've ever tried.

THREE HOUR BONERS?

Remaining rock hard for one, two, or even three hours is a lot easier and more natural than it sounds. The trick is, there really is no trick. There is no expiration date on your boner. There's plenty of blood circulating your body to keep your soldier standing at attention for as long as you're having fun. Time will pass and you won't even think about how long it's been. You've actually been a sexual Superman all this time and didn't even know it. Orgasm was your kryptonite.

If you run into erection problems, look at your diet, your weight, your sleep habits and your lifestyle basics. Medications can cause blood flow problems. Avoid meds with sexual side effects unless it's a life or death issue. The benefits you get from Karezza sex will far outweigh the benefits of any non life-sustaining medication you take. Also try lifting weights and reducing your body fat.

Erections are a pretty accurate gauge of your overall health. The better your health and fitness, the stiffer your boners will be. If you need a boost, the amino acids L-arginine and L-citrulline are excellent for men's health and erections. These natural supplements work similarly to prescription erection drugs in dilating your blood vessels for optimal blood flow throughout your body (heart, brain, muscles, lungs, and penis).

Besides these general erection health tips, there's nothing special you need to do to have sex for 3 hours vs. 10 minutes. As with all physical endeavors, the better shape you're in, the more you'll get out of it. That's another reason to get and stay fit, gentlemen. While not an absolute necessity for Karezza sex, fitness definitely takes it to the next level.

CHAPTER 3:
NO NUT: PREVENTING ACCIDENTAL ORGASMS

"One should mount a woman as if riding a galloping horse with rotten reins or as if fearful of falling into a deep pit lined with knife blades. If you treasure your sexual energy, your life will have no limit."

- The Su Nu Ching

At some point on his Karezza sex journey, every man faces difficulty avoiding ejaculation and orgasm. This goes double for guys who are sexually inexperienced or have a new partner. It can also happen to men in long term relationships. At times, the mere idea of being inside a gorgeous naked woman feels like too much.

You can do everything right, but occasionally your balls still feel like they want to explode. Fortunately there are a variety of techniques and approaches discussed in this chapter that can eliminate nearly all accidental orgasms. This matters because once you start retaining your orgasm, there's nothing worse than having your retention streak broken.

The benefits of retention accrue over time - weeks and months. But they can be wiped out in a flash. While one accidental nut doesn't necessarily bring you back to square one, you'll lose much of your accrued 'superpowers' - your focus, your motivation, your confidence, your energy, your libido. To put it plainly, this feels shitty.

THE SEXUAL ENERGY MINDSET

The bedrock principle for avoiding accidental orgasm is to approach each Karezza encounter with the right philosophy and outlook. Adopt a *sexual energy* mindset. Get interested in the flow of sexual energy between you and your woman. This is the real beauty of Karezza sex where you can get lost for hours in layer upon layer of previously untapped sexual awareness. This magic lifts both partners to a higher plane - an experience that resonates for days and weeks. It's also the type of sex where you're less likely to cum.

With dedication and lots of practice in the bedroom, you'll learn to transmute your animalistic urges to a higher chakra (in Hindu terms), creating a more spiritual and sustainable sexual energy. This is how you stay out of the orgasm danger zone. In Taoist terms, rather than channeling sexual energy toward climax, you retain it to replenish your life force and invest in higher pursuits.

Compare this to the *fucking* mindset of most orgasm-sex encounters. Karezza sex really is different. Hell, it's a whole new reality. And yet, overlap exists between the animalistic and the spiritual approaches to sex. Sometimes being fully present, mindful, engaged, and loving can actually *intensify* the urge to orgasm and ejaculate. Preventing that from happening takes practice, awareness, and a very solid bag of tricks.

STAGES OF AROUSAL: TWO PATHS

The first step in preventing accidental orgasm is developing awareness of your arousal and the path it takes. Your sexual energy is a beast, but you are a beastmaster. Recognizing when and where the beast gets unruly and learning to reset its focus will make the difference between a fruitful Karezza session and that sinking feeling of having just jizzed all over the place.

The first stage of arousal is a boner, getting hard. We've all been there a million times. The next stage of arousal is *pleasure*.

Pleasure is that wonderful feeling you get sliding your penis into a warm, wet pussy. You get the picture. The pleasure stage of intercourse can last for a while, especially if your sexual energy is nice and strong but not overflowing. It's a pleasant and peaceful feeling of renewal, hope, love, strength, and freedom. But beware. The pleasure stage is fueled by raw energy and all raw energies yearn to manifest in a more finite form.

The next stage of arousal presents a fork in your hero's journey to Karezza fulfillment. On the path more traveled, the next stage is *lust*. That road ultimately leads to orgasm. On the path less traveled, the next stage is *bliss*. This road ultimately leads to peace and fulfillment.

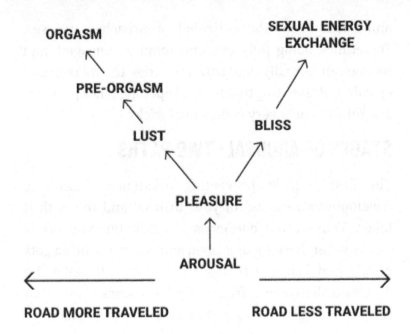

ROAD MORE TRAVELED   **ROAD LESS TRAVELED**

THE ROAD LESS TRAVELLED

Heading toward Karezza fulfillment, the next stage after pleasure is *bliss* (see diagram). Bliss is where sexual excitement migrates from the penis to full diffusion throughout your body. This is the core of what people love so much about Karezza sex. The feeling is one of complete flow with nature, with your purpose, and with universal sex energy. Not your thing? It will be once you try it. It's the sex you already love - but so much better.

Sustained bliss eventually leads to a sense of complete energy exchange and sexual fulfillment (see diagram). How do you know when that's occurred? Ideally, it's the point where you're still quite aroused but there's a profound, calm sense of total satisfaction - and you can tell your woman feels the same way. For more on sexual energy exchange and successfully finishing a Karezza sex encounter see *Chapter 8: Finishing: Are We There Yet?*

THE OLD, WELL WORN PATH

In orgasm-sex, pleasure leads to *lust* (see diagram). Lust is the stage where your juices start flowing, your behind-the-scenes equipment engages, your gun gets locked and loaded. Technically you're not close to cumming yet, but all systems are on standby. In most cases, lust quickly leads to the next stage of arousal - *pre-orgasm*.

If lust is the danger zone, *pre-orgasm* is the war zone. But lust doesn't mean orgasm is inevitable or that success is out of range. With some practice the skilled Karezza gentleman can maneuver his way back to *pleasure*, then attempt the manifestation again, this time to bliss.

Pre-orgasm is when you're so fired up the pleasure is very near physical ecstasy. You can hover in and out of this range for a while, but it's unwise. Similarly to masturbatory edging, it's a pure thrill play. The longer you taunt yourself on the edge of orgasm, the more overwhelming the perceived *need* for orgasm becomes - even if it's totally subconscious. If you spend enough time in this "war zone" your retention streak will eventually be the casualty.

The good news about pre-orgasm is that you can back up and still have a successful Karezza encounter. Take a break. Lay in bed for a few minutes, hold hands, contemplate the mysteries of the universe together. Tell each other what you're grateful for about each other. Cool all the way back down to baseline arousal. Visualize the energetic exchange you aim to achieve. Consider how long it's been since your last orgasm and how much that means to you. Consider what pride you take in giving your woman an amazing sexual experience while demonstrating in the most raw, animalistic terms possible how highly you value your seed, your purpose, and your role as a strong leader.

If you feel ready to go back in for another run at perfect energetic exchange, you're a good man. Go for it. But if you find yourself repeatedly ramping back up to pre-orgasm despite your best efforts, it might be time to throw in the towel for the night.

KAREZZA SEX VS. SEXUAL EDGING

While it's possible to successfully back up from pre-orgasm and recover your control, don't make this your regular routine. Intentionally steering toward pre-orgasm then slamming on the brakes is sexual edging.

Deliberate sexual edging isn't good for your body, mind, or energy. Teasing your fluids all the way to release then stopping at the last moment is unnatural. Sexual edging abuses your prostate and balls, disrupts your mind by leaving you unfulfilled, and frustrates your sexual energy by keeping it pent up and stuck.

This isn't to suggest you should go ahead and ejaculate if you accidentally end up in the danger zone. Don't do that. But don't get caught up in the thrill of edging either. Accidental edging will happen occasionally and that's normal, but intentional edging is a profound distraction from the true magic of Karezza sex.

The best way to avoid arriving at the edge of orgasm is to redefine your own personal "edge" as the fork in the road where pleasure splits off into either lust or bliss (see diagram above). This way, you'll train yourself to course correct well short of the actual edge any time you get off track.

PREVENTING ACCIDENTAL ORGASMS

Once you understand the stages of arousal, it takes some practice to get into perfect flow and avoid accidental orgasms. Fortunately if you know the warning signs, learn your triggers, and practice some basic techniques you should consistently be able to avoid *the point of no return.* Later in this section, you'll learn an advanced technique to stop an orgasm dead in its tracks once it's started.

KNOW THE WARNING SIGNS

The next step in preventing accidental orgasm is to become aware of the warning signs. As orgasm approaches, you may feel some or all of the following: movement in the balls and prostate, heart flutter, shallow or heavy breathing, muscle contractions, loss of control, a slight lump in your throat. These are all signs your body may be getting ready to spring an orgasm on you.

The body wants what it wants, and it tells no lies. If you pay attention to these subtle signs and even more obvious ones such as leaking pre-cum you'll know when it's time to cool down, at least for a while.

KNOW YOUR TRIGGERS

On your Karezza sex journey, you'll become aware of personal triggers that can provoke orgasm. It could be something she says, or a certain way she touches your hair, face, or body during intercourse. It could be a particular way she moves her body or something special she does with her vagina during sex. It could be a thought that pops into your head.

Each man has different triggers and they shift and change over time. If you suddenly feel yourself lurching toward pre-orgasm when you thought you were comfortably in bliss territory, try to figure out what sent you there. The next time she says that thing or moves that way, you can be ready for it.

CYCLES OF HORNINESS

Maybe it's the weather, maybe she's ovulating, maybe you just had a big success and feel unstoppable. There are a million factors that can spike your testosterone and libido and put you at higher risk for accidental orgasm. We can't always identify every trigger, but we can recognize when we're going through a cycle of extreme horniness.

When you're feeling extra horny, be aware of it and make a mental note. Be honest with yourself about any triggers that are within your control. Have you been looking at sexy pictures or videos? Whatever the reason, give yourself a pre-sex pep talk in the mirror. Remind yourself that you're in a state of higher than average horniness and to be mindful of all your tools to prevent orgasm.

SLOW DOWN AND BREATH DEEPLY

One of the most effective techniques to walk yourself back from lust or pre-orgasm is to simply slow down and breathe deeply. Ever notice how most orgasms don't occur during the slow part of sex? When orgasm is impending there's an instinctual tendency to go fast.

Going slow instead of fast can often change the course. In fact, Karezza sex is often called '*slow sex*'. While Karezza sex does not need to be exclusively slow, there is something about slowness that facilitates control. It gives you that much more time to be aware of small shifts in energy and make corrections as warranted. Breathing deeply further connects you to the moment and enhances your ability to regain control.

RELAX YOUR PC MUSCLES

During orgasm, our pelvic floor (PC) muscles contract like crazy. This triggers the prostate to spew semen. These PC muscles are located along your perineum aka your taint or gooch (see graphic below).

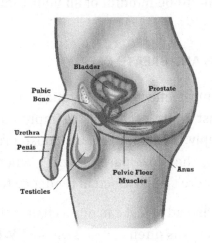

As sex intensifies, we have a tendency to contract and flex these muscles as excitement builds. This makes us feel manly in the animal sense because it engages the prostate/balls framework in anticipation of a potential reproductive episode. Before we know it, we're fired up and nearing pre-orgasm.

Next time you have sex, try to become aware of your PC muscles and you'll notice this dynamic at play. Building the mind / PC muscle connection is one of the most valuable keys to unlocking Karezza sex mastery. Once you're aware of these muscles, you can relax them at will. This technique is your passport from pleasure to bliss.

Men who need help relaxing the PC muscles should look into magnesium glycinate, which is great for men's health overall: heart, mood, sleep, body composition, blood pressure, and erections. It's also a natural muscle relaxant ideal for easing subconscious PC muscle tension during sex. Be aware, however, that too much magnesium can cause fatigue so moderation is essential.

FLEX YOUR OTHER MUSCLES

Spiritual sex doesn't preclude animal expression. Guys who work out and are in tune with their muscles know there are a million different ways to flex and engage your arms, your core, your chest, your back, your shoulders, your legs, your hips, your glutes, your neck, and even your face during sex.

Flexing and engaging these muscles during sex is a great way to experience full body sex, physically express your masculine energy, and subvert the instinct to express that energy through orgasm.

THE BLOCK (ADVANCED TECHNIQUE)

Sometimes you do everything right to steer away from orgasm and avoid engaging your balls and prostate, yet the unthinkable happens: an orgasm starts from out of nowhere. Maybe she caressed your penis with the walls of her vagina in a way you didn't know was possible. Maybe the reality that you're having sex with a woman just gets *too real* for a second.

Usually what happens next is we go into defense mode. A low-key state of panic sets in - especially if you're on a long retention streak you don't want to break. Maybe we pull out, maybe we boldly stay inside her but 'park it' for a minute. Usually, slowing down confirms we were only on the edge of orgasm - on the safe side of the point of no return. Other times, even without any further stimulation it just starts to... *happen*.

You might read elsewhere about manual techniques to stop an impending ejaculation. You might read about choking the emission off where your cock head meets the shaft. You might read about a so-called 'million dollar point' you can manually jam along your perineum to stop an ejaculation dead in its tracks. You won't find such techniques endorsed in this book because a) they raise some health and safety concerns b) these techniques often allow for orgasm even in the absence of ejaculation - whereas the benefits of retention come largely from avoiding orgasm and c) there is a better way.

Once you've reached *the point of no return*, your mind is your only true ally. Fortunately, there is a way to use your mind to stop an *orgasm-in-progress* dead in its tracks. It's called The Block.

First, a caveat: you must have strong delayed gratification skills to pull this off. Here's where those weeks and months of working out, staying on your purpose, eating right, avoiding porn, minimizing social media, etc. will work in your favor.

The key to blocking an orgasm-in-progress is to quickly and authoritatively establish mental dominance and control over the would-be orgasm. Here's a dirty secret you won't read anywhere else: orgasms feel passive but they actually *require our participation.* It's a rare man who can close his eyes, stare down the most aggressive animal in the world just as it's about to feast on its favorite meal... and beat that fucker into submission. But it's not a rare man who can *learn* to do this.

The trick to applying The Block successfully is to make the rock-solid decision that IT'S. NOT. HAPPENING. Period. End of story. This is no ordinary decision. It's war. Before sex even begins you must fully commit to the belief that orgasm is the enemy. That way when it sneaks up on you it won't feel like an old friend stopping by for a long overdue visit.

When a surprise orgasm rears its ugly head, here's what to do: Stop everything (pull out if you haven't already) and scream the loudest, most intense mental "NOOOOOOOO!!!!" inside your head. You should almost scare yourself with how aggressively you attack and kill this lesser beast called orgasm. Don't worry about what's happening with your cock and balls. Ignore your body. You may leak a small amount of fluid - it's no big deal. Just focus on mentally *murdering* that orgasm and stopping it dead in its tracks.

The next part requires a leap of faith and tremendous belief in your own power. You must allow yourself to let go of the physical plane and delve headfirst deep into the realm of raw energy. The Block occurs in a hypnagogic, almost psychedelic dimension of awareness. You will be transported for a split second to another realm of reality where you will have the opportunity to slay the orgasm dragon. If you're wholeheartedly determined at that moment, you will succeed. An ounce of doubt or weakness, and you fail.

The mental fortitude required to pull this off can be likened to the strength Superman uses to spin the earth backwards to turn back time. It's an intense power that is more godlike than human. *But it is possible.* The key is to refuse any participation whatsoever. If you cede even a millimeter of territory here - if you enjoy it for even a nanosecond - you will fail. The Block requires an iron will.

Make no mistake, The Block is by no means a pleasant experience or something to take on lightly. Your eyes will roll back into your head. You'll look and feel as if you're having a stroke. You may see stars flashing, like being knocked out. You'll be nonverbal. Afterward, you'll feel catatonic and half alien - like you've been to another world, fought in a battle royale, and come back a different man.

And then.... you'll feel more awesome and alive than you've ever felt before in your life. Because *you did it*. You established dominance over the most powerful animal appetite of all: orgasm. You took on the beast directly and won. You're one of an elite few men who cannot be stopped by anything.

And you executed this powerful display of leadership and dominance right in front of your woman. She may admire you already, but wait until she's witnessed you successfully deploy The Block. She will be in awe, and rightly so. There's no better way to demonstrate to your woman how committed you are to retaining your energy and staying on your path.

THE ROAD TO MASTERY

The Block isn't just a failsafe technique. It's actually the gateway to mastery. Once you've successfully executed it, an entire new world of sexual possibility gradually presents itself to you. Knowing you have the ability to prevent orgasm relaxes you. Soon, you'll learn to "pump the breaks" a bit at a time - applying microdoses of the requisite mental energy when you feel yourself veering toward lust or nearing the edge.

These microblocks become part of your everyday practice. Over the course of a few months, The Block becomes a constant mindset, ingrained in your awareness, always available. This is your gateway to mastery and total control.

Eventually, you will graduate to the point where it becomes second nature. Like using the breaks on your car, you don't think about it, it just seems to happen. The only time you'll need to consciously apply the technique is in rare circumstances where you get extremely close to the edge. The rest of the time it'll take care of itself.

This is the road to mastery and greatness because it frees you up to experience the joys of sexual energy flowing throughout your body and spirit without the stress of possible orgasm. Karezza sex is very pleasurable and fulfilling even before you attain this level of mastery, but once you do it becomes heaven, zen, and nirvana all rolled into one.

THROWING IN THE TOWEL

Some days might you feel like a stud horse whose mission in life is impregnating females with your seed. You feel it in your soul. You tried to do everything right but all you want to do is fill that vagina with your ooey-gooey genetic code. This is normal. If you're feeling this way on a particular night despite doing everything right, it's probably time to wind the encounter down. In fact you can even use it to your long-term advantage. Your woman will melt when you say that her beauty and sexiness is making it nearly impossible for you to hold back your seed but that you must.

When you feel yourself hovering in and out of pre-orgasm, despite good efforts to channel your energy elsewhere, call it a night. Later, take a moment to ask yourself if anything you've been doing lately could have contributed to your orgasm mindset. A frequent culprit might be sexy pictures on social media. Or it may just be something in the air. Or a full moon. Or spring fever. Whatever it is, don't risk accidental orgasm. Call it a night. Occasionally, you may even need a day or two away from sex to cool down and recalibrate your energy, but with practice this will happen less frequently.

ACCIDENTAL ORGASM

Like any valuable skill, Karezza sex takes practice to master. Meaningful progress involves making some mistakes. Along your Karezza sex journey there may be a few accidental orgasms and ejaculations.

When you're spending such massive amounts of time with your penis inside vagina, sometimes nature's reproductive framework outsmarts you momentarily. Shake it off, brother. It's not the end of the world. It's all part of the process. If you read and absorb even a fraction of the techniques, strategies, and solutions in this book you're already light years ahead of men who are trying to figure Karezza sex out on their own.

PRO TIP: DON'T ENJOY IT

Here's an advanced tip to mute the negative effects of an accidental orgasm. Don't participate. Don't enjoy it. Don't give in to the pleasure. Let it happen if you feel there's no other way, and if you haven't yet mastered The Block (discussed above). But don't enjoy it. Don't thrust or touch yourself. Just let it happen and move on. This is the opposite of the type of advice you'll find in 99% of books, but it makes an enormous difference. The less pleasure you take in an accidental orgasm, the less likely it is to happen again.

AFTERMATH

Once you have a taste of Karezza sex, orgasm is no longer a thing of great pleasure. You don't care about that so-called reward anymore - you're too busy having the best sex of your life. An accidental orgasm feels strange and can be upsetting. You instantly feel your energy take a nosedive. You lament the loss of your retention superpowers.

Do yourself a favor and don't focus on those negative feelings. These slip ups typically don't happen very often, so when they do, it's better game to mine them for a) lessons to be learned (what was the trigger, what can you do differently going forward) and b) the silver lining.

THE SILVER LINING

The silver lining to an accidental orgasm is that while retention is the *best* state of being for a man, it's not a *perfect* state. Seeing or visiting 'the other side' is an experience that an intelligent man will mine for great insight.

If nothing else, it's a sobering reminder of the cloudy mental state of 99% of the population who are hooked on orgasms. Focus on the huge advantage Karezza sex gives you over those people. Think about how quickly you will regain that advantage over the coming days, weeks, and months.

There's undeniable value in getting knocked down and climbing back up even higher. We're all part of the universe and sometimes the universe wants to teach us a lesson. Be man enough to learn it with humility and a sense of humor.

RECOVERY

Successful recovery from an accidental orgasm demands an active approach. The most important piece of the puzzle is to analyze what went wrong and visualize yourself successfully navigating a similar situation next time.

Feeling you're not in control of your orgasm and ejaculation is disempowering and can reduce your confidence in bed, in your relationship and in other aspects of life. Fortunately, regaining confidence doesn't require perfection. It only requires you take the bull by the horns and get the situation under control: monitor it and take active steps to improve it. Other things that will benefit a speedier and/or smoother recovery include: vitamins, exercise, clean eating, plenty of sleep, and progress on your life goals.

THE BIGGER PICTURE

Some guys get pretty upset about slip-ups. It's understandable. Nobody likes them. A planned orgasm is one thing, if that's how you roll. But an orgasm you tried with every ounce of your being to avoid is the worst. Losing control of your ejaculatory function in front of your woman is humiliating. But here's the bigger picture: *most guys do it every time they have sex.*

And most women will never even once go to bed with a man who's so dedicated to his purpose in life that he literally fucks without cumming. The big picture is that if you're even *trying* this, you're already a legend. Your legendary status will only be enhanced (not diminished) when you recover from your slip-up and rise again as the sexual hero you're determined to become.

CHAPTER 4:
KAREZZA TRANSMUTATION
(HOW TO PRINT MONEY IN BED)

"The meaning of the word transmute is, in simple language, the changing or transferring of one element, or form of energy into another."

- Napoleon Hill

KAREZZA SEX: THE ULTIMATE SUCCESS HACK

There are a few different reasons people are typically drawn to Karezza sex. Some are drawn to the relationship benefits, others to the spiritual element. Many others (especially men) are drawn to Karezza as a means to success. As Napoleon Hill pointed out in his 1937 classic Think and Grow Rich, sexual transmutation is one of the top success hacks used by great world-shapers and visionaries.

Karezza sex is the ultimate tool for sexual transmutation. More than that, it's also a mental training ground for success. During Karezza sex, a man trains himself to sustain a feeling of dominance in the absence of immediate reward - even when gratification is far down the road, if ever. This is the *exact* mindset required to achieve big and meaningful things in today's complex and competitive world.

Hey baby, mind spending an hour in bed with me tonight? I need to train for success so we can build an even better future. It might sound far-fetched, but this is the way many couples start to think once they give up orgasm and learn the benefit of channeling their sexual energy toward their goals.

SEXUAL TRANSMUTATION

Sexual transmutation is letting sexual energy flow through you without sexual release. Instead, you express that triumph, creativity, and love through another outlet.

Sex energy is so raw and fundamental that it can be channeled toward higher pursuits quite efficiently. Yet this energy is so insanely powerful that most men never learn to harness it and cash in on the potential riches. Sexual transmutation isn't exactly easy to do. Yet, as the many men who have mastered it can attest, it's not that hard either. And it's well worth the effort.

There are <u>three steps</u> necessary for sexual transmutation: 1) Cultivate sexual energy 2) Retain that sexual energy and 3) Apply that sexual energy toward your goals. Today's world presents challenges on all three fronts.

Men's testosterone levels are a fraction of what they were a few generations ago. There is a severe shortage of male sexual energy in our society. Plastics, pesticides, pharmaceuticals, alcohol, obesity, sugar, entertainment, and social media all suppress men's sex energy and drive.

Men who are fortunate enough to avoid these traps (or young enough to not yet feel the effects) often deplete their sex energy as quickly as it builds up - through frequent orgasm. It's no wonder men are statistically falling behind. Between suppression and waste, 99% of men today have very little sexual energy available to transmute.

STEP 1: CULTIVATE SEX ENERGY

The first step in sexual transmutation is cultivating sex energy. Without sexual energy, you could hold your seed forever to very little benefit. If the river is dry, channeling it in another direction won't bring water there either.

Cultivating sex energy in today's toxic environment is a 24/7 lifestyle. But that doesn't mean it's time consuming or even expensive. It's all about your habits.

INNER GAME

To cultivate sexual energy, your head must be on straight. Make sure your surroundings are orderly and neat. Declutter the information you allow into your mind. Limit your consumption of news and media that doesn't tie into your purpose in life. Limit your participation in groups and activities that don't directly tie into your purpose and stimulate your growth.

Quit porn and masturbation. Porn and masturbation seem to offer a jolt of sexual energy (and they do... sort of), but they lead to orgasm which means spilling your seed. Porn also puts you squarely in the spectator seat. In fact, porn cements the idea in your head that you are a mere beta boy, not worthy of sex yourself, relegated to the rank of a spectator who can't even keep his hands out of his own pants.

Porn and masturbation are not approximations of sex - they're the opposite of sex. They don't make you strong or give you energy. They make you passive, weak, and unattractive to women. They make you a bitch.

Meditate, or at least spend some time in quiet solitude. Get out into nature, near the water, and around animals. Listen to instrumental music like classical, jazz, cinematic, or electronic. Lack of lyrics helps quiet and focus your brain.

Expose yourself to constructive content and positive people who are solidly on their own purpose. Force yourself outside your comfort zone as it pertains to your goals. Stake out new territory. Set targets and experience wins.

EAT RIGHT

Eating right is essential to efficient cultivation of sexual energy. Avoid sugar and artificial sweeteners, junk carbs, and processed foods. Eat organic produce or peel and rinse your fruits and veggies to avoid pesticide exposure. Eat clean. Get plenty of protein.

Phytoestrogens in food can destroy male sexual energy. Some of the biggest culprits are soy and soy-fed meat, flax seeds[2], dried fruits, sesame seeds, multigrain breads (which usually contain lots of seeds), legumes, chickpeas (including hummus), and pumpkin seeds. While men require a certain amount of estrogen, our bodies convert testosterone into estrogen as needed. The problem with phytoestrogens is they trick your body into shutting down its own testosterone production because it thinks that's where the extra estrogen came from.

EXERCISE AND WELLNESS

In addition to eating right, it's important to give your body all the important vitamins and minerals. It's almost impossible to do this through diet alone unless you're a multimillionaire with a personal chef. Take a high quality multivitamin. Supplement additionally as needed. Vitamins C and D and minerals like zinc, magnesium, and boron are conducive to cultivating male sexual energy.

Building muscle stores sexual energy in your body and creates mental strength and fortitude. To build muscle, consistently eat high amounts of protein and do at least bodyweight exercises (pushups, calisthenics, etc.) every day. Lifting weights is even better. Over time your body will change and become the lean, muscular body type that makes the perfect vessel for male sex energy. You

---

[2] A note on flax seeds: they are in almost every 'health' food these days. Avoid them like the plague. They have 3.5 times the amount of phytoestrogens compared to soy.

don't need to get huge, the idea is to build lean muscle mass over time.

AVOID TOXINS

Daily exposure to toxins is one of the biggest threats to your sexual energy. As much as possible, limit your interaction with plastic and artificial fibers. Don't believe the hype around BPA-free and other so-called 'safe' plastics. Nearly all plastics contain endocrine disruptors that render male sex energy less potent.

Opt for one hundred percent cotton or other natural fiber clothing where possible. Wearing polyester (or anything that sounds chemical or estrogenic) is like wearing a low-dose estrogen patch against your skin on a daily basis. Not good for cultivating male sex energy. Likewise, limit exposure to commercial soaps, lotions and fragrances - all of which have this same effect. Use something natural instead. Also make sure your drinking water is free from fluoride and other toxic additives and contaminants.

CHECK YOUR MEDS

Optimizing your sexual energy requires a critical look at any pharmaceuticals you take. A few medications significantly improve real life-or-death conditions. Most don't. And many medications list sexual dysfunction as a side effect. These prescriptions snuff out your sexual energy. They kill your sex drive. But without sex energy, there can be no transmutation.

If you're on meds for a chronic condition - do some research. Are there alternatives with less sexual side effects? The answer could be a different drug or even going the natural route with diet, supplements, exercise, and meditation. Consult your doctor before quitting any long-standing regimen, but do your own homework. If your doctor says you can't have both health and virility, get a second opinion.

Many men today take antidepressants, anxiety drugs, and ADHD medications. These pills may improve symptoms but don't cure the underlying existential crisis. They don't give your life *meaning.* Orgasm retention injects your life with meaning. You start to feel it right away and it gets stronger daily. A close, committed Karezza relationship gives your life meaning. Karezza sex has the potential to make anxiety, depression, and ADHD a thing of the past. And it's a lot more fun than taking pills.

THE KAREZZA EFFECT

Having sex cultivates more sex energy. It sounds too good to be true, but it works. However, orgasm releases this energy as quickly as it builds. Sex without orgasm builds and stores unlimited amounts of sex energy - the raw material of transmutation. This is the big advantage of Karezza transmutation. It's an unlimited fountain of pure sex energy.

STEP 2: RETAIN SEX ENERGY

The second step in sexual transmutation is retention. Before you can transmute and apply sexual energy to your goals, you must master retaining it. How do you retain sexual energy? The answer is simple: no orgasm. No nut. It's that easy.

Boiling water creates steam. Your steam can fly away and become worthless. Or you can harness it to power an engine and create electricity. Imagine letting all your steam fly away and go to waste instead of using it to power your ideas and inventions.

Sounds preposterous, yet most men do this every day. When pressure builds, they let it off through orgasm. Their engine never runs. They never generate an electric spark. The great tragedy of our time is that men don't understand their own potential - or how easy it is to attain once you opt out of orgasm and retain your sexual energy. Karezza sex makes retention a sustainable practice. It allows you to fully enjoy sex without sacrificing your steam.

STEP 3: APPLY SEX ENERGY

The third and final step in sexual transmutation is applying your sexual energy toward your goals. Application of sexual energy is two pronged: it requires you 1) have a purpose and 2) put in the work.

Sexual transmutation doesn't chart the course for you, do the work for you, or make success easy. Yes, sexual transmutation gives you an almost superpower-like ability to channel your hard work into something valuable and impressive. But the rest is up to you.

YOUR PURPOSE

The first element you need to apply your sexual energy is a purpose. Your purpose is your outlet for all the sexual energy you cultivate and retain. Your all-consuming objective or project. It needs to be more than *doing great at my job* or *being a great guy*. It should be personal, it should be challenging, it should be something that takes time to master.

It could be a business, it could be a skill, it could be a crazy idea or goal that you have. It should tie into the direction you want your life to take. Since it's all-consuming it must directly serve your overall vision for yourself and your life.

We become what we do. If you don't have a purpose yet, make it your purpose to find one. In the meantime, also make it your purpose to build a set of daily habits that make you stronger.

Pro Tip: Don't make women your primary purpose. Some guys believe they need a girlfriend before they can excel in life. Fair enough. Some men tolerate being alone better than others. We're all different. But even if you make finding a woman one of your top priorities - don't make it your main purpose. You must have a purpose bigger than getting your dick wet, even if it's in the world's finest pussy.

A word of warning: if you don't have an all-consuming purpose (or make it your purpose to develop one) transmutation is pointless. You will end up releasing your seed out of desperation or you will douse your own sexual fire through low-level distractions like video games, alcohol, social media, and entertainment. Once you decide to transmute, you must take action and follow through on your purpose. There is no other way.

A purpose is essential to sexual transmutation, but it's not enough. The final ingredient is productive action. Hard work smartly targeted toward maximum progress. Orgasm retention and Karezza sex will lead to genius ideas and valuable insights. But without action, these strokes of genius are worthless.

Don't retain and just wait for the results. There will be none unless you put in the work. Success takes work. Work takes energy. That's where transmutation comes in. *Transmutation gives you the energy to do the work.* Karezza sex creates unlimited amounts of this energy.

A DIRTY SECRET

Here's a dirty secret. Your sperm and your balls *know* that excelling at your purpose will eventually attract pussy toward you. *That's what transmutation is all about.* That energy, that seed needs to get out into the world. You deny it masturbation, it wants pussy. You refuse to chase pussy, it finds a way to attract pussy to you.

Once you get pussy, you deny yourself release, then what happens? Your seed and that sexual energy will work to make you greater and greater until women are literally lined up around the block begging to have your baby for the sake of humanity. It sounds like an exaggeration, but it's not much of one. That life force, that reproductive energy is the most powerful force in the world.

Every time we level up in life, we gain a reproductive edge. Evolution demonstrates this on a grand scale. Sexual transmutation is you and your seed working together for your mutual benefit. But while your seed is all powerful, you can't let it lead the way. Remember, you're the daddy. Your seed is less than a baby. So why do 99% of men let their seed run the show?

HOW TO PRINT MONEY IN BED

Karezza sex is so beneficial for a man's ability to succeed, that once he masters it he might as well have a machine in his bedroom for printing money. It's *that* effective - and a hell of a lot more fun than operating a printing press.

Nothing stokes and harnesses the full power of your seed (procreative drive) like the gentlemanly art of Karezza sex. When you perform Karezza sex you tell your sperm: *You want to come out? You want to swim up inside a pussy and make a baby? Here, I'll get you close. Let's hang out in a vagina for a while.*

You literally give your seed a sniff of what it wants more than anything. But you don't let it out. What does your seed do in response? It dials your drive up another notch. And then you transmute again. Giving your seed constant whiffs of the inside of a pussy, letting it get physically so close to those eggs it wants to fertilize, raises your sexual energy through the roof. Mastery of this art raises a man's self-confidence and overall feeling of dominance. Success will flow your way as the universe rewards your discipline. This is how to print money in bed.

THE STORY OF THE YELLOW EMPEROR

Sometime around the 4th Century, an ancient text emerged in China: The Su Nu Ching. Unearthed and translated by Douglas Wile in his 1992 book *Art of the Bedchamber: Chinese Sexual Yoga Classics*, The Su Nu Ching presents a dialogue between The Yellow Emperor and fertility goddess Su Nu. The degree to which it mirrors our current understanding of orgasm retention and sexual transmutation is remarkable.

When the Yellow Emperor inquires about the consequences of avoiding sex altogether, Su Nu replies that this would be a mistake. If you avoid sex, your spirit has no chance to expand, she explains. When yin and yang are cut off from one another, you become weak. Su Nu advises cultivating energy through frequent sex. Then she divulges a secret. She says the proper method of sex is frequent intercourse but without ejaculating. She proclaims that this makes a man healthy in a hundred different ways.

The Yellow Emperor, of course, wants to know more about the advantages of sex without orgasm. Su Nu explains that retention sex one time strengthens a man's Qi energy. Two times, it improves your sight and hearing. Three times, makes you healthy as a horse. Four times, it fortifies your vital organs. Five times is good for the heart. Six times strengthens the core. Seven times, it strengthens the legs. Eight times, it makes you glow. Nine times earns you longevity. Ten times... and you become immortal.

THE INTENSITY AND HOW TO HANDLE IT

With orgasm retention comes a fierceness, a vigor, a potency, and intensity. It increases with time. The longer you go, the more it ratchets up. Of course, this is exactly what most men are looking for when they pursue sexual transmutation - it's one of the top benefits. But it can also be tricky to moderate this intensity and act like a regular human being when the occasion arises.

The number one way to handle the intensity is to relentlessly channel it into active pursuit of well-defined goals. Keep working. If you don't have a purpose, an all-consuming goal or project, you will struggle with the intensity. Get in the habit of running your life like a business.

Even when not working, staying active is key. You won't feel comfortable watching TV, you won't feel comfortable idly chatting with boring people. Get plenty of exercise. Lift weights. Clean and organize. When you want to relax, prioritize enriching activities like yoga, meditation, reading, playing music, creating art, getting ample sleep, and communicating with stimulating people.

And of course plenty of Karezza sex, since it's the perfect opportunity to take some of your excess extreme yang energy and pass it along to your partner. This exchange energizes your woman tremendously and she can only get this from you so it's a gift and a service you should be happy and proud to perform.

KAREZZA TRANSMUTATION: A MUST IN TODAY'S WORLD

Orgasm addiction makes you weak. It makes you passive. It makes you a baby who will do anything to get back inside a female body and blow your load. Orgasm addiction makes you easier to sell to, easier to manipulate and easier to control. It's the meaning of that infamous truism: *sex sells.* Orgasm addiction makes you emotional. It makes you impatient and dependent on instant gratification.

Why do we accept this as inevitable? The predominant message most young men hear growing up is that frequent ejaculation is healthy, their seed has no value, their sex organs are 'junk', and nothing beats instant gratification. If you're older than 14 and not cumming at least 5 times a week there's something wrong with you (and let's be honest: most guys do it far more than that). That's the message. It's not hard to see why sexual transmutation is still on the fringes of polite conversation. There's nothing polite about rejecting societal norms.

And yet, after many centuries the transmutation movement is finally starting to take off in earnest. Why now? Because there's just no other viable way anymore, gentlemen.

To beat the distractions, pollutants, and overwhelming mediocrity of today's world, transmutation is no longer a luxury - it's a necessity. Life is more complex and competitive than ever, but it's also more full of opportunity. To take advantage of these opportunities you must be your best.

Sexual transmutation is powerful and it works. Harnessing its power puts you ahead of the pack because they don't have the discipline. Karezza sex takes the power of transmutation and turbocharges it with a perpetual supply of rocket fuel. Karezza transmutation is regular transmutation on steroids - your checkmate in the game of success.

CHAPTER 5:
HOW TO TURN ANY WOMAN INTO YOUR KAREZZA GIRL

IT TAKES TWO

So you've decided to give Karezza sex a try. You're willing to trade the fleeting pleasure of orgasm for a more fulfilling and happier life, a better version of yourself, and more success. You want to try sexual transmutation and try "printing money" in the bedroom. Perhaps you've been retaining solo and feel ready to graduate to the big leagues and loop a woman into the process. Time to get out there and have some fun.

That's the spirit! But how and where do you find a Karezza girl? And if you already have a woman, how do you turn her into your Karezza girl? After all, women like orgasms - a lot. Everywhere you turn women are discussing their orgasms. It's become a status symbol among women to not only have orgasms but to proclaim them loudly. Yes, women are just as brainwashed as men about sex these days. Orgasm has become just another drug, a form of enslavement. Women are hooked on it as badly as men.

So how do you find a woman who's willing to go on this crazy journey with you? It's not as hard as you might think. Good women are *starved* for strong men. Good women are thirsty for quality, masculine men who live out their purpose. Our culture's energy has become predominantly feminine. That's great news for masculine men - because we're in very short supply and scarcity equals value.

Karezza sex is the most masculine act you can perform for a woman. Think about it. Your hard cock inside her pussy. Pretty masculine. Driving her wild with pleasure for an hour or two. Quite masculine. Demonstrating the value of your seed by refusing to spill even a drop. *Ejaculate? That's for boys. I'm a man.* Masculine as fuck.

Women crave this type of masculinity. A woman will worship the man who lovingly introduces her to Karezza sex. And she'll follow your lead, provided you follow the techniques and strategies outlined in this chapter.

TO FIND A WOMAN, BUILD THE MAN

Finding a woman for a Karezza relationship is quite different than finding a girl to just hang out with and fuck. You want to look for an authentic connection, an energy match, something with potential. To find that, focus on cultivating your own masculine energy rather than studying pickup lines and techniques. Salesmanship is important in dating, but it should be the icing on your attraction cake, not the main ingredient.

Feminine energy is largely innate, while masculine energy must be cultivated by the man himself. This is the paradox of yin and yang. Until you cultivate yours, you have nothing to exchange and women will be hard to find.

The #1 way to attract quality women is to make yourself into a man you're proud of. Why would you even deserve a woman if you don't have any concrete achievements to be proud of? Accomplishment builds self-esteem, pride, and masculine energy. This energy attracts high quality women. It can't be faked or brought about by anything other than struggle and achievement.

Become good at something worthwhile and you won't have any problem finding a woman. Work on your physique, your career, or special skills that take time and effort to master. Nothing is sexier to a woman than a man with self-discipline. Why? Because he's a proven leader. He's proven he can lead *himself* and that's something most men can sadly never claim.

Many men mistakenly feel they need to trick a woman into dating them, hence the popularity of pickup systems. This mentality is based on the flawed premise that women hold all the cards because they are the ones being pursued. But in reality, she is not superior to you - she just happens to be what *you* need. But you're also what *she* needs. *You each need each other equally.* Keep this in mind and 99% of your women problems will disappear.

Hone your value and masculinity, then let nature and energy take their course. This process doesn't typically take long. Your accomplishments don't need to be earth-shattering. You can build momentum you're proud of in a few short months. Taking the time now to get your masculine energy right will lead to nearly instantaneous results once you start actively pursuing women. They'll see your value, feel your energy, and fight tooth and nail for you. In fact, don't be surprised if they start chasing you first.

KAREZZA SEX WITH A NEW CONNECTION

Karezza sex with a brand new connection may seem daunting, but in truth it's a great opportunity to show up and establish gentlemanly leadership in the relationship right off the bat. It's also a good way to filter out women who might not be a match for a man like you, who's invested in personal growth.

WHEN TO BRING IT UP

Men looking for a Karezza girlfriend might find themselves debating when to bring up their interest in Karezza sex. The answer is it depends. Generally speaking, when interacting with women, it's important to show up as a man and wear your sexual interest on your sleeve. But that doesn't necessarily mean discussing the particulars of sex right away. Flirtation and other less overt forms of sexual interest can be appropriate and effective ways to get the sexual dance started and test each other's chemistry and responsiveness.

Your interest in Karezza sex isn't a dirty, shameful secret you're hiding from her. But the best salesmen know you must put your prospect at ease and establish trust and emotional leadership to get them in the buying mood.

Let it come up naturally. In some connections, that might be on the first date. Maybe she's very into sexual spirituality or personal development or wellness and Karezza sex seems like the perfect conversation topic. In that case, don't hold back. Every woman is different and every connection is different.

The main thing to remember when you bring Karezza sex up is: *it's no big deal.* Karezza sex is just the type of sex you're interested in because it feels heavenly and makes people happy and successful. Your tone should be enthusiastic yet straightforward, simple, and matter-of-fact.

Women are attracted to strong, loving leadership. That's precisely what you're offering. Don't be afraid she'll think you're weird. Don't be afraid of anything. Women need men as much as we need women. They're also hungry for a good match with a solid partner that enhances their life. And good sex.

Yes, she'll probably feel it's a little crazy-sounding. But she'll also be excited to talk to a guy who thinks differently, fucks differently, and separates himself from the pack. Which reaction ends up dominating in her mind is completely up to you. Show up as that exciting guy and you'll both be glad you did.

SPRING IT ON HER IN BED?

Here's a scenario. You've had a couple dates with a woman. You really hit it off. The chemistry is palpable and you want to explore it some more. She's coming over to your place tonight. You both know what that means. But you haven't had a chance to mention Karezza sex yet.

You consider just taking her to bed and simply not cumming. Maybe even making her orgasm first before winding down. Then casually mentioning you don't do orgasms. Bad plan.

This woman just gave herself to you completely, had an orgasm in front of you naked and vulnerable and spread wide open. Now you're telling her you're too good to do the same? That's ungentlemanly and potentially hurtful to the girl. The right thing to do is discuss it before you hit the sheets.

If you can't have a conversation about sex with someone you probably shouldn't be having sex with them at all. This is where you grow up and become a man. When sex becomes the elephant in the room, something you both really want, it's your job to initiate a conversation in the most chill and respectful way possible.

THE TALK

When it comes time for the talk, keep it low key. Don't make it seem like you were expecting sex. Sure, these days everyone is expecting sex after a date or two (if they even get that far) but a gentleman treats sex as something earned, not owed. Bring it up in a straightforward way. *"I'm feeling some strong sexual energy and attraction between us. It feels really great and I'd like to explore it further with you."* This is different from what men usually say and it will intrigue her. Put it in your own words, but the point is: find an enlightened way to steer the conversation toward sex.

Avoid the *'I've got something to tell you'* serious vibe, as it unnecessarily puts you on the defensive. You're not telling her about a raging STD, or that you're actually a sex offender, or that you prefer to be the receptive partner during intercourse. You've actually got *great* news for her.

Pro Tip: Before you tell her about Karezza sex, let her do some talking about sex herself. Ask her some questions to get her going. *"Sex can be really personal and we've never talked about it. What are some of your thoughts or feelings about sex?"* Depending on her personality, she may have a thoughtful response or more of a giggly and shy one. It doesn't matter because either way you 1) showed her that you value and respect her thoughts and opinions and 2) created a sense that it's okay and normal to have diverse ideas and opinions about sex.

Follow up with questions like: *What do you think about sex in today's culture? What do you think about orgasms? Do you think sex is more about the journey or the destination? Do you believe in spiritual sex and healing sex? Have you heard of sexual transmutation?*

The follow-up questions you ask will depend on where the conversation goes. The overarching goal is to open up a conversation and create a dialogue on your philosophies about sex... and then to reveal *your* philosophy within the context of that conversation. By being non-judgmental and interested in her thoughts on sex, you model and invite her to do the same in return when you tell her your thoughts.

You know when the last time was that a guy had this type of conversation with her before sticking it in? Never. Because they were orgasm-addicted boys. That's the Karezza sex advantage, gentlemen. It's the ultimate way to set yourself apart as a higher value man in the bedroom and in life.

REGULAR SEX FIRST?

If you haven't had Karezza sex yet, you might logically decide to do the following: find a girl you like, get the relationship and the sex going and then a couple months down the line spring Karezza sex on her. This can certainly work if you have the skills and the confidence to pull it off, but it's tricky for a few reasons.

First, you'll feel like shit jizzing all over the place when you really want to retain. Once you understand the power of orgasm retention and Karezza sex, it's hard to spill your seed, even as a means to an end. It feels wrong.

Second, it builds up one type of sexual connection when the type you want is completely different. In other words, it's a waste of time and energy. Don't waste months cumming because you lack the balls to take the sexual lead in your relationship.

Third, starting out with regular sex you'll spend a couple months in "honeymoon mode" where the sheer newness of the connection confers a special excitement. Then around the time you're planning to phase out orgasms, the relationship is also losing its newness factor. So you end up *taking two things away at once.* Not a well-thought-out or gentlemanly thing to subject a woman to.

Ideally, it's better to start off with Karezza sex, but for some guys it's overwhelming. Some guys also find it very difficult to hold their fire the first couple times with a new connection. If that's you, don't worry. You can start with regular sex. The key is to then transition to Karezza sex as quickly as possible - within days or weeks, not months.

This part is tricky. Something about new pussy seems to suck the sperm right out of your balls. All you can do in this situation is your best. But know this: it is one hundred percent possible to retain successfully even with a new woman. Your mind *can* achieve total mastery over your nut.

On the other hand, if you've been retaining for a while and the reality of having your penis inside a woman is *just too much* and you bust accidentally... rest assured you're still doing the right thing. Growth requires you take risks. It also requires learning by doing. The psychological benefits of sexual and romantic victory far outweigh a few short-term blips in your retention streak.

One of the goals of your retention practice was probably to find a woman. So if the shear excitement of having sex makes you prematurely ejaculate a couple times, look at it as an opportunity to prove you can roll with the punches, get knocked down, get back up and not be destroyed. Then follow the tips in *Chapter 3: No Nut: Preventing Accidental Orgasms* to cement your Karezza sex retention game.

FINDING A WOMAN WHO'S ALREADY INTO KAREZZA SEX: PROS AND CONS

Another option is to find a girlfriend who's already into Karezza sex and who could maybe even teach you a thing or two. This eliminates the need to explain it to her and also eliminates your need to learn the ropes for yourself because you have a willing teacher. With the right woman, there could definitely be some benefit to this strategy, but it might not be your go-to approach for a couple of reasons.

First, there aren't a lot of women out there who know about Karezza sex. There are a few places online where you can meet them but your available pool of women will be pretty small. On the plus side, you'd already have something in common. But to find a good match, many men will want a bigger pool of women to select from.

Second, you must consider whether it's healthy to enter into a relationship where you're sexually submissive to the woman. You as the sex student, her as the sex teacher. In most healthy relationships, the man takes charge in the bedroom and thus in the relationship. This is not to say he has total control. How he navigates the relationship outside the bedroom determines whether she wants to keep going to bed with him. There's a balance of power, a harmony of yin and yang.

Putting your woman in charge of the sex program gives away your opportunity to establish gentlemanly leadership in the relationship. Some guys can navigate this successfully and effectively reclaim their standing after a few Karezza sex lessons. But sex energy is powerful stuff, so you'd better know what you're doing.

The news for this option isn't all bad, however. A respectful, loving, nurturing sexual mentorship could be a beautiful experience. An example might be a shorter term Karezza sex mentorship with an older woman. You acknowledge her as a woman and teacher and she acknowledges you as a student and as a man who fulfills her need for male sex energy. There is a balance of power. Starting a long term relationship this way is more challenging, but worth exploring if the dynamic strongly interests you or gets you particularly rock hard for some legitimate reason.

FROM HARD MODE TO KAREZZA KING: A ROADMAP

A growing number of men abstain from masturbation and sex altogether (aka *'hard mode'*). These are the retention kings, the men who soldier on under their own power despite lack of exogenous sex energy.

When this man decides to level up with Karezza sex, he'll do great because he's already developed his delayed gratification muscle. This also gives him the patience to select a good mate - not just one he thinks he can rope into Karezza sex quickly.

We all want to get naked with a woman, but it's worth taking the time to find the right woman first. Hard mode, no-porn guys have the rare ability to do this. Then, when you find the right girl, simply use the tips in this chapter to introduce Karezza sex into the relationship.

Hard mode guys who make the leap to Karezza sex generally report great benefits. Quitting orgasm without eventually taking advantage of the Karezza sex technology is like becoming a violin virtuoso but never playing with the orchestra. You're on the right track, but you're missing out on something celestial and otherworldly - a profound reorganization of individual elements into a breathtakingly beautiful whole.

KAREZZA SEX FOR VIRGINS

If you're a virgin and plan to start off your first sexual relationship with Karezza sex, congratulations. You are a man among men. Your level of sexual restraint is admirable. Now it's time for some pussy. Every man needs it sooner or later and now you're ready.

Whether or not to tell her you're a virgin is up to you. If you tell her, be proud of it just like you're proud of your interest in Karezza sex. Ideally you can bake the virginity disclosure right into the talk you have with her about Karezza sex (see "The Talk," above).

Don't make a big deal out of the virginity thing. Yes, it's a huge moment for you. But you're a man and you're ready. Every man before you had his first time and we all made it. You will too. If you have this attitude she'll find it very attractive and you'll enjoy yourself a lot more, because male sexual energy is all about confidence.

It's also legitimate *not* to mention you're a virgin. After all, it's a lot of responsibility to put on a girl's shoulders which could inhibit her enjoyment. Sometimes the more gentlemanly thing to do is keep your inner giddiness to yourself and act as confidently as possible. Karezza foreplay will give you ample opportunity to finger her pussy and get the lay of the land. You've seen porn[3], so you know the mechanics. And remember, this shit is meant to be instinctual. Animals figure it out, you can too.

When the time comes to put it in, make sure she's plenty wet *(see Chapter 6: Jing Juice: Taoist Wet Pussy Secrets)*. Rub some spit over the head of your cock to make sure your first entry is smooth and pleasurable for both of you. If any of this goes awkwardly, don't worry. She's probably nervous too and didn't even notice.

If she is also a virgin and her hymen is intact, you will need to pop her cherry on the way in. This doesn't require any special technique, but may cause her some initial discomfort and bleeding. Be supportive, be gentle,

---

[3] Not an endorsement of porn, but an acknowledgement most of us have watched it.

be loving, and savor the experience with her. It's a beautiful moment for both of you.

Everyone is nervous with a new connection, not just virgins. If you feel the need to acknowledge a particularly awkward fumble or misstep, just chalk it up to her being so sexy you're trying to stay really focused on not busting a nut. Beyond that, follow the Karezza sex tips in this book and you're well primed for success.

Whether or not to tell a new connection you're a virgin is up to you. It's a tradeoff: the intimacy of honesty vs. the confidence of not saying anything. It can work either way. Virginity is nothing to be ashamed of, but you can determine whether losing yours should be more of a group project or an individual pursuit.

CASUAL KAREZZA: PROS AND CONS

Some men may believe the logical way to start their Karezza sex journey is to keep it casual - to train themselves in retention sex without the pressure of building a romantic relationship at the same time. This might be a legitimate approach for certain men, but there are some issues to consider first.

KAREZZA SEX VS. RETAINING DURING CASUAL SEX

There's probably no such thing as truly casual Karezza sex. Karezza sex is about more than just orgasm retention. In fact, it's about more than sex. Here's a secret you may have already picked up on: *Karezza sex is really about energy.*

Retention is merely a mechanism to trigger abundant awareness and exchange of sexual energy. The more this energy is purified and fortified with love and intimacy over time, the more clean, potent, and useful it becomes. That's where a strong relationship comes in. You don't need to be a hardcore Taoist to notice the difference between loving sex and impersonal sex and the impact it has on people's lives.

Karezza sex leaves you feeling sexually satisfied. Your horniness is transmuted to motivation and genius. The slow, intimate, loving connection of Karezza sex relaxes you and facilitates transmutation. This is very difficult to achieve during impersonal encounters. And without transmutation, your sexual energy will get stuck, increasing your restlessness rather than energizing you.

EXAMINE YOUR MOTIVATION

Karezza sex can be tricky. It's not hard, but there's a learning curve. You may make mistakes. But do you really need to practice with throwaway pussy before finding your true Karezza girl? Does your future partner expect - or even want - you to be perfect at it in advance?

There are energetically cleaner ways to learn the ropes. You can visualize yourself practicing retention sex[4], you can watch videos where people describe their experience, or you can read about it - which you're doing right now. These activities prime your mind for Karezza

---

[4] Visualization only, no hands. Quitting masturbation is a prerequisite for Karezza success. If you need help, get an accountability buddy or accountability coach.

success without compromising your sexual energy through impersonal encounters.

If you get so horny on retention you feel the need to go out and smash some strange pussy - you're a man and that's your business. But be honest with yourself about your motivation. Are you focused on the energy or on the ass? Is it training for Karezza sex or just having fun? Maybe it's both and that's okay too.

True Karezza sex is very fun, but it's by no means *just having fun*. The problem for men with 'just having some fun' is it channels your sexual energy into finding more novel sex partners instead of what else you could accomplish with that time and energy.

STRANGER DANGER

Every sex partner is a stranger at first, even if we've been on a few dates or known each other a while. Having sex with a stranger is very exciting on an animal level. But serial pursuit of this thrill is the enemy of love. Only love purifies your sexual energy for efficient and powerful Karezza sex transmutation.

We all need pussy in our lives. But pussy is everywhere, like the oxygen and water we also need but don't freak out over. Pussy is just as plentiful as air and water. There will always be pussy, and pussy will always need dick. Finding a way to fit this exchange into your life in a healthy way makes a man great. Serially chasing fresh tail dissipates a man's energy and holds him back in life.

During sex we share our most primal energy. The way we treat and respect this sexual energy plays out in our daily lives. It's important to conserve this energy and not spend it indiscriminately.

Often, men forget that women have a different sexual experience than we do. During sex, women make themselves vulnerable to receiving our male sexual energy which we broadcast inside them. If your sexual charge is coming from a positive, loving, and growth-centered place then you're giving the woman a wonderful gift. If your energy is coming from a cheaper, lesser place, that's not a great gift. Wielding the yang energy in the sexual transaction is a great power that also comes with great responsibility.

SHORT TERM AND EXPLORATORY RELATIONSHIPS

Avoiding casual sex doesn't mean you need to be married before hitting the sheets. Sex is an appropriate step to take at some point in your new relationship. And relationships don't always work out. Some relationships end up being short-term. That's normal.

What matters is your intention. Did you go into the relationship seeking a real, open-ended connection or did you create a false connection in order to lock down a short-term practice partner? Your intention will determine the quality of the energy you exchange. The purer your intention, the better it will transmute.

5 CONCRETE STEPS TO TURN YOUR CURRENT WOMAN INTO YOUR KAREZZA GIRL

If you're already in an established relationship, turning your current girlfriend or wife into your Karezza girl is a fun and rewarding process that will deepen your connection like nothing else. It's typically pretty easy, too. In 95% of cases, the following five simple steps will do the trick. If you apply these strategies and methods, Karezza bliss will be yours.

STEP 1: SHOW HER THE ROPES

Whether or not to discuss Karezza sex before giving your woman an in-bed demonstration depends on the nature of your connection. In many established relationships, you can skip the pre-discussion before having Karezza sex for the first time.

Unless she's very prone to easy orgasm herself, it's entirely possible to introduce this new style of lovemaking with your actions rather than words. To achieve this, simply lead by example by shifting to slower, controlled, Karezza-style intercourse and when the time feels right, suggest winding it down without orgasm.

If your relationship is a good fit for this approach, the benefit is that she's already enjoyed Karezza sex before she even hears about it. Then when you discuss it later, she's already invested. If you're a solid leader and closely in sync as a couple, this approach can be quite intriguing to a woman and turn her into your Karezza girl rather quickly.

On the other hand, your particular couple dynamic may compel you to discuss things first. Or you may be justifiably concerned that without a pre-discussion she'll orgasm, which will make it harder to hold your own fire.

Whether you talk before or after, keep the initial discussion low-key and confident. Let her know you want to give sexual transmutation a try because there are a lot of benefits. Emphasize the benefits you think will appeal to her most, like the relationship ones, or maybe income.

Unless you've been talking about this stuff for a while, transmutation will sound pretty crazy to most women. The less you make a big deal out of it, the easier it will be for her to buy in. Your woman wants to follow you, but only if you act confident. *No big deal. Same great sex - just more of it and sweeter.* Boom.

When the topic of whether orgasm retention works for women comes up, tell her you've heard it's great for women too. Let her know it's up to her but you think it's worth a try and you're here to support her. Say it would be a fun thing to do together. At this point, she'll typically agree to at least a trial run.

Women long for romance and sexual adventure. Every woman's secret dream is to follow her strong man down a road of passionate sexual trailblazing. Awakening this fundamental desire in your woman will likely be much easier than you think.

STEP 2: LEAD THE WAY

Once you switch to Karezza sex, the intercourse becomes mind-blowing - certainly better than any she's had before. She will be happy about that. Make sure she sees you having a lot of fun and enjoying it too. Casually mention how great you feel and the benefits you're enjoying.

Some men might be moody when they first quit orgasm as the addiction subsides. Do your best to keep your cool around your woman during this phase. If you lose your cool, be straightforward and humorous about struggling a bit, emphasizing that the long term benefits will far outweigh temporary moodiness.

At this point if your woman has any sense of adventure and romance she's likely ready to become your Karezza girl (at least in the back of her mind). Just keep selling it. You already sold her on trying it, just take it a step further.

STEP 3: BECOME HER SEX GURU

The next step is to become her own personal sex guru. Share your knowledge and insight about sexual energy and transmutation. This book gives you plenty of knowledge to drop on her sporadically. Be her sex genius. Sprinkle in some Taoism and some of your own personal observations. Every man is a philosopher.

This is where you start to carry yourself like a man who doesn't follow the pack. This is where you become a man who values his own opinion. This is where you flex your masculinity. Build your muscles, deepen your voice, grow your beard, or learn a badass skill. In other words, do whatever it takes to stand out as a leader worth following.

Becoming a strong, masculine leader serves an important purpose. It allows your woman to detach from the mindset of her friends, family, and co-workers. Women value agreement and consensus. With Karezza sex, you are asking her to disagree with everyone she knows regarding sex - and to agree with you instead. That's where stepping up your game and establishing guru status comes in.

Act like someone worth leaving her old mentality behind for. Be her hero. She'll love you for it. They tell little girls not to believe in heroes anymore. Imagine how happy you'll make your woman by transforming into one right before her eyes. If she's not fully on board yet, she will be soon.

STEP 4: GIVE IT TIME

Time is your best friend in this process. What seemed crazy to her when you first mentioned it a few weeks ago, won't seem so strange once she's been immersed in it for a while. The point of this step isn't to wear her down but to give her the time she needs to adjust and shift her agreeability from what everyone else says about sex to the truths you are now teaching her.

Every woman comes from a different background and set of experiences, so patience is a must. If you keep at it, you'll get there. Eventually, she will follow your lead. This is nature's way, the law of men and women. Since you're leading her in a good direction, you can take great pride in persuading a woman to join you on your Karezza sex adventure.

STEP 5: REWARD HER EFFORTS (IN HER LANGUAGE)

Maybe she's 100% on board, maybe she's not. But whatever effort she makes (such as trying one session without orgasm), make a big deal out of it. Women love to be verbally acknowledged. Tell her how close and intimate it feels to you to be doing this together. This isn't bullshit. You *will* feel that way. Just because men don't normally express themselves that way doesn't mean we can't.

Let her know how much you loved connecting with her - how unbelievable it was. If she goes a few days without orgasm, tell her about any positive changes you notice. This isn't insincere. There *will* be positive changes, all you have to do is notice them and express that to her.

Women love to be noticed and appreciated. You should sincerely appreciate every step she takes down this path with you, because it will enhance both your lives tremendously. Let her know that. This verbal encouragement, combined with the other four steps, will ultimately turn any woman into your Karezza girl. Well... *almost* any woman.

4 QUESTIONS TO ASK IF SUCCESS ELUDES YOU

Following the above steps will turn almost any woman into your Karezza girl. If success eludes you, there are a few logical possibilities as to why. Asking yourself these four questions will often get to the heart of the matter.

Is your energy mismatched? Karezza sex won't create a spark where there is no chemistry to begin with. In most cases, Karezza sex brings couples closer together, but if your relationship was shallow and your sex had been largely thrill-based, you may find when you go deeper that you're not a match.

Is she immersed in the trashy side of culture (porn, pop culture, trash social media, etc.)? Common sense should tell you not to get involved with a woman like this. She's not ready to think outside the box. Her loyalty is to the *culture* - not to you, not even to herself or her own best interests. If you really have a thing for this girl and want to pursue it, you must be a strong and bold leader who can turn her interests around. Even then, you're in for a bumpy ride, but nothing is impossible.

Is she addicted to orgasm? The initial days and weeks of retaining her orgasm may hurt like hell for her at first. Be a leader and be supportive. Anticipate her needs. Remind her that she's *trading up* not *giving something up*. Let her know It only takes around two weeks to get past the worst effects of orgasm withdrawal. Be her prince while she endures the pain. With your help, she can do it.

Is she operating at a lower frequency than you? Perhaps she just lacks the ambition to better herself or try something different. Maybe she's happy enough with her orgasms and doesn't see what the big deal is. Normally, you can excite a woman into following your lead, but if she can't be excited consider the possibility she's just not on your level.

THE RARE HIGH QUALITY WOMAN WHO WON'T DO KAREZZA SEX

95% of women will follow you into Karezza sex if you follow the 5 STEPS. 95% of the rest fall into one of the four categories above - energy mismatch, addicted to culture, addicted to orgasm, or lacking ambition. But what about that rare *high quality* girl who doesn't want anything to do with Karezza sex?

Maybe you have an amazing girlfriend, great sexual spark, great values and personality match. You like everything about her. Her personality and attitude are a ray of sunshine and positivity. She inspires you to get out of bed in the morning. She's fiercely loyal. She's gorgeous. You honestly have no complaints about her at all. If this is your situation, it's probably worth exploring one-sided Karezza sex. See how it works for you. That's how the Taoists did it, after all.

There have always been two schools of thought regarding whether women benefit from retention to the same degree as men. Anecdotally, women report great results from orgasm retention. The more we learn about orgasm's effects, the more it makes sense that women benefit greatly. The power of delayed gratification applies to both men and women.

But if your woman is too good to be true, don't kick her to the curb just because she enjoys the occasional orgasm. Of course it's possible you will grow apart eventually, but when the universe puts the 'perfect' woman into your life, one potentially winning strategy is attempting to work with what you have and make the best of it. If her orgasms turn out to be a deal breaker, at least you gave it your best shot.

IF SHE DOESN'T WANT YOU DOING IT EITHER

Most women take to Karezza sex like bees to honey. A few women won't do it, but they're mostly women you don't want. Very occasionally, you'll run across a woman who doesn't even want you retaining *your own orgasm*. Why would a woman demand this? There are a couple common reasons.

She may fear you won't cum with her because she's unattractive or otherwise unworthy of your seed. If this is the reason, go out of your way to show and tell her how gorgeous and sexy she is and reiterate how much you are doing this for her and for your future together. She should come around.

On the other hand, maybe she fears she'll lose her grip over you without the power of orgasm. Maybe she sees you becoming stronger and more independent and doesn't like it because she's afraid you'll outgrow her. Having this reaction doesn't make her a bad person. But if it makes her dead set against Karezza sex, she's likely a bad fit for you.

Never let your woman dictate your sexual practices (or any deep conviction) when you have determined and charted the best course already. Take her opinion into account of course. But if you let a woman control you like that, you become submissive in the relationship and everything that can go wrong from there eventually will.

A good woman should never try to hold you back, she should always try to build you up. In turn you should make it known to her that you are not planning to outgrow her and that you want to grow together. If a woman can't respect this and can't accept your personal Karezza sex practice, it's time to move on.

WOMEN ARE EVERYWHERE

Finding your Karezza girl or turning your current woman onto Karezza sex is a fun, noble, and highly rewarding process. It calls on you to be a man in every sense of the word: a leader and lover in the bedroom and out. You'll need to demonstrate patience, love, and an unwavering commitment to your goal.

Your interest in Karezza sex sets you apart and differentiates you from other men. They all want the same thing. You want something different. Something better for you and better for her.

Many high quality women will respond with excitement and willingness. Some women won't. The women who respond are the ones you want. They're the women all men want, but most men never break away from the pack enough to excite these high quality women.

Your interest in Karezza sex is a great screening tool to avoid the wrong women and attract the right women into your life. Be a man, be a leader, retain your orgasm and semen, cultivate your masculine energy, relentlessly pursue your purpose, and you may not even have to go looking for these women. They might just flock to you.

CHAPTER 6:
JING JUICE: TAOIST WET PUSSY SECRETS

VAGINAL LUBRICATION: THE SCIENCE

When it comes to facilitating smooth and pleasurable sex, sufficient vaginal lubrication is key. You can't fuck a dry pussy. But how does a gentleman get a woman's juices flowing? Men and women have very different warm up times when it comes to physical readiness for intercourse.

For many men, the mere idea of impending sex gets them hard. For others it's a woman's touch or kiss, the site of a woman's naked body, or a woman's hand on his cock. For a healthy, fit man with sufficient libido it usually doesn't take much to get hard in the presence of a woman. Nature takes its course.

A woman's process of arousal is more gradual and nuanced. A woman's arousal is cultivated rather than turned on/off like a man's. That's not to say there aren't times a woman gets instantly wet. For some women this occurs quite often. But you can't take it for granted and expect it every time.

The juice itself doesn't actually flow from inside the vagina but rather from two sets of glands: The Bartholin Glands (on both sides of the vaginal hole) and the Skene Glands (near the urethra) generate the moisture necessary for pleasurable intercourse.

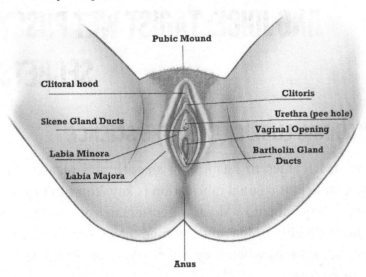

THE TAOIST'S DIRTY SECRET: JING JUICE

Ancient Taoist sex manual The Su Nu Ching advises on the importance of female satisfaction. It reveals vaginal juices are an indicator the woman is emitting Jing (life force). Yes, the ancient Taoists had a dirty secret: wetness is simply the physical manifestation of a woman's essential Jing energy. It's literally Jing Juice. Vaginas are literally fountains of Jing energy.

Su Nu recommends that men use this Jing to increase their own Qi (vitality). Without adequate Jing energy from your woman, transmutation will sputter. Jing Juice is the essential first ingredient in Karezza transmutation.

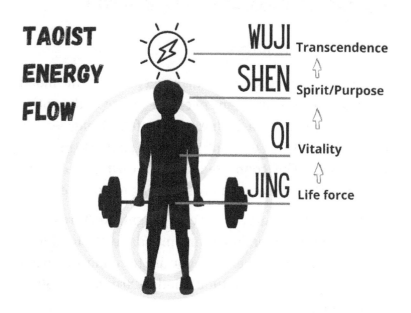

TAOIST ENERGY FLOW

WUJI — Transcendence

SHEN — Spirit/Purpose

QI — Vitality

JING — Life force

THE WET PUSSY TEST

To determine how much Jing energy your woman is emitting, use the wet pussy test. Before intercourse, use her wetness as a barometer for whether her energy is primed for Karezza sex.

During sex, use her continued wetness as your guide to expressing your own sexual energy. If you proceed too aggressively without properly cultivating her feelings of intimacy and feminine arousal, her pussy will run dry during an elongated session. But If you do it right, she will just keep getting wetter and wetter.

5 STEPS TO MAKE AND KEEP HER WET

STEP 1: THE RELATIONSHIP

The first step in making a woman wet is setting the mood far in advance. This means over the course of the entire day and week. Be a loving, respectful, strong leader. Create a culture of gentility and support in your relationship. This connectedness and caring establishes a baseline intimacy that allows her Jing to flow freely.

Even if you have Karezza sex every night, don't treat it as just another habit or something mundane. Let her know earlier in the day how excited you are to connect with her tonight. Cultivate a gratitude mindset around sex. She'll pick up on it.

Do something nice or thoughtful in the hours before Karezza sex. Make her a snack, give her a surprise hug or smooch. Making her feel loved and desired will keep her Jing energy active all day long, primed for juicing.

Male sex energy is a physically penetrating force. Female sex energy is an emotional sucking-you-in. And we do get sucked in, which is a beautiful thing. The flipside is, if you don't have genuine affection for her, she'll feel the energy is off.

When she allows you to physically penetrate her, but you don't allow her to emotionally suck you in, the balance is off - the exchange is uneven. *The Jing Juice won't flow abundantly.* Your transmutation will suffer.

Let yourself get sucked in. Give in to this magnificent power of hers. Let her bring out your loving side. When it's time for sex, you'll both reap the rewards.

STEP 2: FOREPLAY

Foreplay is where you will hone your Jing juicing skills. This is where the magic happens. While visual stimulation is very important to most men, touch and talk are more important to women. A woman loves being touched all over. It gives her a sexy sense of being inspected by the gentleman who'll take stewardship of her body over the next hour or so.

Make her feel loved and respected during foreplay. Women don't know how to act sexually anymore. The predominant message directed toward them online is: be a slut and act like a porn star in bed. For most women this is putting on a performance - it's not how they really want to feel and behave. But what's their alternative? Very few men today are interested in helping a woman develop her true sexual potential. Most men watch porn regularly and their idea of healthy sexual behavior is warped beyond recognition.

Karezza sex is your chance to be that one in a million guy to one special girl. Exert firm leadership that makes her feel valued and loved. In response, she will generate pure, clean, powerful, flowing Jing Juice.

Touch her everywhere. Touch her head, her hair. Her arms, her legs, her tits, her belly, her back, her ass. If her pussy isn't wet enough for fingering yet, place your palm gently over it and apply very light pressure - just enough to warm her up and create a subtle sense of: *knock, knock,*

115

knock, I'm coming in. Keep it there for a while or come back to it intermittently. Her body will respond.

STEP 3: BROADCAST YOUR AROUSAL

Your cock broadcasts yang sexual energy. Make your penis the elephant in the room she can't ignore. This should be done subtly. Don't slap your dick in her face or anything obnoxious and degrading. Such moves don't generate pure, loving Jing Juice.

Let it press prominently against her, let it humorously obstruct your foreplay. Create a sense of *this thing is starting to get in the way - we'd better find somewhere to put it.* This will subconsciously signal her Bartholin and Skene glands that it's time to get wet.

STEP 4: WET TALK

Verbal communication is very important to women and this holds true in bed. Women are aroused through the ears. The trick is to do sexy talk not cheap and dirty, but in a loving, sexy way. To her, this is so much hotter and gets her Jing Juice flowing. Be masculine and direct, yet speak her language. Whisper in her ear or speak conversationally. Be sincere and authentic.

Women crave this type of communication during sex. Many guys avoid it because it takes them out of the moment. Even the most refined gentleman may get a feeling of *let's shut up and fuck* when his woman wants to talk during sex. Change your thinking on this and reap the rewards. Mastering this art keeps the Jing Juice flowing and the heavenly pleasure going and going.

I love you so much... I respect you so much... I find it so sexy that you are so great at everything you do... I admire you so much... You are so incredibly beautiful... I love watching you relax and enjoy yourself in this way... I am so grateful for you... The sexual energy between us feels so amazing, doesn't it?... I love being naked with you, it feels so right... We are such a sexy pair... I love being intimate with you in this way... All I want out of life is to be with you like this every night... Everything else I do is for this... You have the world's sexiest pussy... You are such a gorgeous fountain of pure Jing energy... You are such an amazing woman... I am the luckiest man in the world to be doing this with you right now.

Those are a few examples of talk that can generate substantial Jing flow before and during Karezza sex. For some guys, a few of these might be slight exaggerations, but the point is to describe how you feel in the moment. On paper it looks weird. But spoken sincerely this approach works magic to release cascades of Jing Juice.

Men don't normally talk like this. That's sexy and intriguing to a woman. Karezza sex sets you apart as a man who approaches things his own way. Nothing is sexier to a woman than that.

Pro Tip: Do your own brainstorming and come up with your own verbal Karezza-isms. Put your own spin on it. Refine your approach based on her reaction. The trial and error process of learning to express yourself in her language can make for a lot of good, sexy fun in bed.

STEP 5: KEEP HER WET

To keep the Jing Juice flowing during Karezza sex, you must continuously cultivate it. That's why Karezza sex tends to be slower. Use her wetness as your guide to ideal speed, intensity, and pacing of the encounter. Maybe she gets extremely wet during a stretch of slower sex, then you match her feminine energy with some harder masculine energy until balance is restored. Then you slow down again and repeat.

Keeping your woman wet for an hour or more requires the strategy and mindfulness of a chess master. What made her gush 5 minutes ago might not keep her wet now. It's your job to figure out what will - if you want to keep going and fully express your sexual energy together.

THE LUBE TRAP

Artificial lubricant should be avoided as much as possible. For an occasional boost, use spit to keep it natural. Artificial lube is helpful in certain cases but it can easily become habit. When lube becomes habit, your woman's ability to generate pure natural Jing Juice atrophies. Her self-confidence takes a hit too, because Jing is the special energy a woman brings to the table during sex. If not for the Jing she emanates, sex becomes merely physical. It loses its soul.

SETTING YOURSELF APART

Cultivating a woman's Jing energy is an art and skill a gentleman should devote himself to on every level - mental, physical, emotional, and spiritual. This investment will reward you like nothing else in the world. And it's easy when you use the techniques in this chapter as your guide.

Most people today barely have the attention span to look away from their phones during sex, let alone the mindfulness to cultivate natural pure Jing energy. Committing to this process is a rewarding and fun way to set yourself apart as a top one percent lover.

CHAPTER 7:
HOW TO BE A GENTLEMAN IN BED

"Karezza sex isn't fucking. It's a fucking way of life."

— Nick Brothermore

WHAT IS A GENTLEMAN

GENTLEMAN (n.): a noble, chivalrous, courteous, or honorable man. The term originates from Middle English which borrowed it from the Old French (*gentilz hom*) in the Middle Ages.

As originally defined, *gentleman* referred to a man of character, nobility, and honor. Counterintuitively, living honorably and nobly often requires men to be anything but *gentle* in the modern sense of the word.

It wasn't until the 16th century the word *gentle* came to be associated with mildness and lack of force. The real meaning of *gentle* has nothing to do with being tender, soft, sweet, or unassuming. Those are newer connotations.

Being a gentleman isn't about being a pushover or less manly. It's about maintaining your own high standards and staying focused on your purpose while you treat people respectfully and operate from a mindset of abundance and leadership.

Being a gentleman is about putting your masculinity to work for you, for your purpose, and for those you care about. It's about cultivating your masculine sexual energy and transmuting it from lower pursuits toward higher ones.

THE GENTLEMANLY ART OF KAREZZA SEX

One important aspect of being a gentleman is treating women right. There's no sport or honor in treating a woman badly. Women deserve our respect and gratitude. For who they are. For the crucial role they play in our lives and in the world. For everything they do for us as men. Women deserve our best and they rise to the occasion when we show up as our best.

Teaching a woman Karezza sex is one of the greatest and most gentlemanly gifts a man can give a woman in today's world. If you think your brain is overloaded with information, notifications, and noise... imagine how she feels. Women are evolutionarily hardwired to be responsive because as mothers they must be. All the noise and information that drives you crazy - she has to work twice as hard to filter it out.

Forgoing orgasm is the ultimate unplugging from the noise of life. The ultimate shortcut and hack to inner peace. Can you think of a more gentlemanly pursuit than leading a good woman out of the land of porn, trash, clickbait, and low level gratification? And toward a new life where she can breathe, relax, and be herself - without the anxiety of needing her next fix? Once you quit orgasm, you no longer feel desperate about life. Are you man enough to give a woman this monumental gift? If not, you should aspire to be.

IN BED AS IN LIFE

Sexual energy is our most raw, basic energy. How we treat it determines how we manage our entire lives. Karezza sex enthusiasts note that sex becomes fully integrated in their lives when they give up the orgasm chase. Sex is no longer just some dirty fun you have for a few minutes a few times a week if you're lucky.

Karezza sex becomes a natural extension of who you are and how you treat people. This spills over into your relationship. You embody your Karezza sex roles in day to day interaction. This takes your relationship to a level of harmony and functionality most people never dream possible.

There's a lot of ungentlemanly shit going down in the bedroom these days. Much of it is inspired by porn. Don't settle for this pale imitation of real sex. Great sex isn't about fantasy. It's about reality. Great sex isn't about mindlessly fucking strangers. It's about mindfully connecting with a loving partner. If it needs to be extreme to be enjoyable or exciting, you're doing it wrong.

Connect with your woman. Revel in bringing two halves of the whole together and staying connected and in sync for a long time. Enjoy the endlessly rejuvenating physical pleasure. Bathe in your woman's pure, clean Jing energy.

Renew your spirit and hers too. Then head out into the world and make great things happen. Challenge yourself and grow, then bring that success back into the bedroom and level up all over again. This positive feedback loop will take you anywhere you want to go in life - and beyond.

WHAT A WOMAN NEEDS IN BED

What does a woman need in bed? A woman needs respect in bed. She needs caring, She needs love. She needs you to acknowledge and appreciate her beauty. She needs to see and feel the effect she has on you. She needs you to create a safe space where she can relax, unwind, be naked, and be herself sexually and energetically.

A woman needs excitement and fun in bed. She needs to feel sexy. She needs you inside her. She needs you to touch her all over, say sweet things to her, suck her tits, and kiss her relentlessly. A woman needs to get charged up with your sexual energy in bed. And she needs to share her energy with you. But she needs to be vulnerable as hell to let that happen. Vulnerability requires trust and intimacy.

A woman needs to feel *what she means to you* in bed. She needs to feel that your relationship means something - that there's potentially a great romantic story afoot between the two of you. She needs to know that your sex is much more than just two people fucking because it's fun and convenient.

A woman needs to believe in something in bed. That something is a good man and that good man is you. A woman needs you to run the show physically and sexually in bed *and* do all the rest of this for her while you're at it. Are you man enough? Are you up to the task? If you've read this far, the answer is surely yes.

INTENSE KAREZZA SEX

What a woman *doesn't* need in bed is for you to hold back your raw masculine energy. That's not to say you should be rough, cause pain, or anything like that. But the act of inserting your penis into a vagina is always a bold one. While many refer to Karezza as *slow sex* (and it is slower), in reality it can also be quite energetic and passionate.

Karezza sex is loving and respectful, yet the intensity and vigor can be quite high - especially when the man has been retaining his seed for a while. What does it mean to be zealous in bed but not rough? It means your woman can feel your intensity. It means she can feel your physical and spiritual masculine energy. It means passionate, intense, mindful, controlled lovemaking.

Intense Karezza sex is very different from the hard pounding you've seen in porn and may have engaged in yourself. Rough sex transmits your sexual energy - but in a disrespectful way because there's no real connection. And if your woman doesn't feel respected, loved, and safe, she won't produce the pure, clean Jing energy that feeds your spirit and gives you the true benefits of intercourse.

That's not to say women don't get wet or excited when men bang them. It may be very titillating and exciting to

125

her, but that excitement is a nervous, anxious, and ultimately depressing excitement. No work, no love, no care went into the act. It's empty.

Intense Karezza sex, on the other hand, is extremely respectful. Respectful of your woman. Respectful of her body. Respectful of her female emotions. Respectful of her female energy. Respectful of you and your male energy. The bedroom is where all the sexual tension that builds up daily between a couple is brought into the open and hashed out. A chance for you to show your woman the utmost respect, but also to put on an awesome display of strength and virility.

Getting in touch with your intense side in bed allows you to later take that energy out into the world and conquer. The key is transmuting your aggression into passionate, respectful sex.

It can be the intensity in your eyes and in your muscles. It can be the way that you wrap your arms around her during intercourse, creating positions where she's literally locked in your embrace.

Intensity also means finding ways to channel dominance through your penis in profound yet subtle ways. This has nothing to do with pounding and everything to do with exploring the rich nuances of the penis/vagina connection. The rewards for channeling your animal drive into this type of mindful, controlled Karezza sex can't be overstated.

DO WOMEN NEED ORGASM?

From ancient Taoism through modern times, many have argued that orgasm is not as detrimental to women as it is to men. Some even claim that women *need* orgasm. But while the benefits of female retention are not as widely documented as they are for men, it makes sense that orgasm retention benefits women too.

Orgasm is the most addictive drug in the world, so everybody should benefit from kicking the habit and restoring balance. Women who practice Karezza sex report similar benefits as men - calming of anxiety, improved focus and motivation, sense of control, and better ability to delay gratification.

As a gentleman, you are the leader. As you proceed on this Karezza sex journey, always be aware of its effect on your woman. A good leader can get a woman to follow him. A *great* leader and true gentleman remembers that what's good for the goose is usually good for the gander, but that your woman is not a goose - or a gander. So check in with her. Observe her closely. Read between the lines. Make sure it's going well for her on every level. If she wants to try an orgasm again sometime, give her your blessing. Just don't let the excitement of giving her one push you over the edge.

Observe the results of her orgasm experiment and lovingly let her know what you've observed. Ask her questions and encourage her to express herself openly. Ultimately, it's unlikely that women need orgasm any more than men do. Helping your woman discover this for herself is a rewarding leg of the journey that will bring you closer together.

DO WOMEN NEED SEMEN?

While we're on the topic of what women need and don't need, let's talk semen. Jizz, cum, the sticky white stuff. Do women *need it*? If swimming in a woman's Jing Juice is therapeutic for you, does soaking up your semen have the same effect on her?

In 2002, a study suggested semen can cure women's depression. If that's the case, is it gentlemanly to deprive her of these benefits?

The answer boils down to common sense. First, take a look at the study in question ("Does Semen Have Antidepressant Properties," SUNY Albany, June 2002). Its methodology and conclusions are shoddy at best. The study asked 300 women whether their male partners used condoms. Then they asked the same women about their mood and rated them on a depression scale. The data showed a correlation: women whose partners do not use condoms have less depression.

Fair enough. Common sense would tell you that a relationship not relying on condoms is probably a more stable relationship. The partners are more likely to be exclusive and not worried about disease. They're more likely to be established, long term relationships. They may be less worried about unplanned pregnancy. There is also an enormous sexual energy benefit from skin-to-skin contact vs. skin-to-latex.

The study's authors instead concluded that vaginal semen deposits reduce depression in women. Their proposed treatment was 'artificial semen' delivered in vaginal suppositories for women to overcome depression. If that sounds like a dystopian nightmare, that's probably because it is.

And yet, there could be a connection. The interaction between semen and a woman's cervix has been proven in other studies to send signals throughout her body. Women, like men, are biologically hard-wired to procreate. Semen may signal to her body, hormones, and brain that she is on the right track to make a baby. This could be therapeutic on many levels. A sense of relief. An improvement in mood.

But then what happens? It's easy to see how repeated semen exposure with no resulting pregnancy might severely frustrate a woman's hormonal and neurochemical balance. A good analogy is artificial sweeteners. They send powerful messages to our brain that we've found dense and efficient energy - sugar. At first our survival mechanism rewards us with a release of serotonin and other neurochemicals that improve mood, as if to say *job well done. We can breathe easy for a moment.'* But then... panic. Because you didn't get any energy. You got nothing.

You tried to pull one over on your system and failed because now your system wants revenge and wants it in the form of real calories. And *a lot of them*, because now your system is confused and doesn't want to take any chances. This is why artificial sweeteners actually make people fatter. Or they make people irritable and crazy if they refuse to succumb to binging on real sweets.

If you replace 'artificial sweeteners' with 'semen without conception' it might explain much of the anxiety and depression women report in their lives these days - a nagging sense that something's just not right. What's more, it's feasible to theorize that repeated exposure to semen that doesn't 'do the job' (result in pregnancy) may subconsciously lead a woman to promiscuity in hopes of getting something 'stronger' from the next man in a desperate effort to balance out her system.

Or it could just make her irritable and crazy. Think about the women you know in your life. Is all that semen and no babies making them a little cuckoo and/or promiscuous? You can draw your own conclusions.

Additionally, there is emerging science that excessive semen exposure may overtax women's immune systems, which react to semen as if it were a virus. This could be responsible for women's higher rate of autoimmune disorders and for the fact that these diseases are on the rise worldwide.

The bottom line: there's no solid science either way but there's a strong common sense argument to be made that it's healthier, cleaner, and more sustainable to refrain from filling your woman's insides with semen unless conception is desired.

A NOTE ON LIBIDO

Libido means how horny you feel, but it's more than that. Libido is strongly linked to overall health. Strong libido is a sign your body and mind are in a good place. Since testosterone is crucial to libido, avoiding habits that disrupt testosterone is key. Get in shape. Pursue your purpose. Tune out mass media. Avoid plastics, polyester, commercial soaps, chemical sunscreens, sweets, phytoestrogens, smoking, drinking, pornography, and masturbation. These tips will substantially improve every man's libido.

Cultivating libido is every man's responsibility. Women have libido too, and it can be quite high. But in an ideal relationship the man has higher libido than the woman. This makes the woman feel desired, pursued, sexy, and beautiful. Every woman needs this feeling.

HOW TO BE A GENTLEMAN IN BED

The secret to great Karezza sex lies in drawing your woman's purest, cleanest, most loving Jing energy out into the open for you both to enjoy. Most women have never had this profound experience, and sadly most never will. Most women will never know what it's like to completely surrender to a good and worthy gentleman who's in it not for the cumshot but for the closeness, the intimacy, the love, and the energy exchange.

These days women - and men - are lucky if they can find a real life human partner who's a decent human being. Taking it to the next level and experiencing transcendent bliss isn't even on most women's radar. They don't know it's one of their options. And yet we all have this potential within us. It's our birthright. Once you try it, it feels so natural and right you'll wish you'd discovered Karezza sex sooner.

Once your woman's Jing energy is flowing, match it in every way with your strong, confident, assertive masculine energy. When a woman feels her pure feminine yin energy countered by your pure masculine yang energy, something magic happens, and you'll feel it too. This is the meaning of connected, spiritual sex.

Great Karezza sex requires the proud embodiment of sexual polarities. This is healing for both men and women because in today's world we are treated as mostly gender neutral. But we aren't gender neutral. To 'succeed' in today's environment, men are forced to become more feminine than is healthy for them. And women are forced to become more masculine than is healthy for them. This is poison to our spirits.

How to be a gentleman in bed is to lead your woman away from the hellish dissonance of our orgasm-chasing gender neutral society. Give her the permission to be a woman, to be herself, to be sexual, and to enjoy Karezza sex in the presence of a good, honorable, strong, noble, loving leader of a man.

CHAPTER 8:
FINISHING: ARE WE THERE YET?

A typical orgasm-sex encounter has a beginning, a middle, and an end. Karezza sex does too, but there's an important difference. In traditional sex, intercourse ends when the man ejaculates. Remove orgasm from the picture and you have more flexibility on how to end your session.

By now you understand that the destination of Karezza sex is energetic exchange and spiritual unity. But how do you know when you've achieved this? What does it *feel* like? How do you finish? How do you know if she's finished? What's energy exchange, anyway? In this chapter, you'll find out.

ENERGY EXCHANGE: WHAT IT FEELS LIKE

All sex is energy exchange. Most people are just too busy getting off to notice. Exchange of sexual energy is a feeling of *getting it out of your system* - and at the same time becoming fully renewed. You'll feel so completely recharged that you're ready to hop off your woman and direct that energy outward toward your worldly pursuits.

Any feeling of lack you had is gone. You've established yourself as part of an energetic whole and now you're ready to physically separate from your other half until next time. This is the feeling you're working toward with Karezza sex. A feeling of unity. Clean, pure energy flowing freely and strongly between the two of you. Complete ease and comfort with yourself, each other, your bodies, and your deep sexual connection. Pure bliss. Ultimate flow.

Karezza energy exchange transmutes sex energy and relieves sexual tension. This can happen at any time during the encounter. After approximately 20-30 minutes of Karezza sex, you typically level up to a higher zone of intimate connection. This zone is highly conducive to energetic exchange. With practice, you can get there even faster, but don't rush. If you force it, you won't be relaxed enough to *let it happen.*

Sometimes energetic exchange is gradual - a process of waking up to the flow and spirit of nature. Other times, it can be very pronounced and forceful - intense like a transmuted orgasm.

Men and women both have male and female energy inside. Karezza sex is about physically, emotionally, and spiritually sorting it out until everything is ordered and in balance. Two equal opposites. This can manifest subtly or strongly depending on the energy levels and the specific energy to be sorted during the exchange.

A SWEET SEXUAL SONG

In music, cadence is defined as "a sequence of notes or chords comprising the close of a musical phrase." In layman's terms, it's the final line or two of a song's chorus. Each Karezza sex session is very much a song and the energy exchange is its cadence.

Like a song, you want your Karezza sex to end on a hopeful and sweet note. Maybe you leave her wanting a little more, leave her wanting to hear it again. Maybe you want to get this sexual song stuck in your woman's head so strongly that she begs for encore renditions nightly. That's certainly a gentleman's prerogative and a more than worthy pursuit.

THE BODY POETIC

Poetry is a language unto itself. It achieves that status by showing rather than telling. Stories tell, poetry shows. During Karezza sex you and your woman perform a poem together with your bodies. When it comes time to wind things down and wrap up, think about the type of poem you've written so far and what kind of poetic conclusion you can steer toward.

You might consider the larger context of your relationship, where your woman is emotionally, what both of you have coming up over the next days, weeks, or hours. Try to sum up the experience with your body, your movements, and your words. Steer toward a higher ideal with a hopeful, forward-looking conclusion. A special kiss, a loving smile, a pinky swear to do it again tomorrow. Come up with something sweet and sexy that will leave her wanting more soon.

SPIRITUAL CLIMAX (ADVANCED TECHNIQUE)

When energy exchange feels very pronounced and dynamic, it can seem very much like a transmuted orgasm or spiritual climax. All the energy comes to a head and is powerfully released upward to a higher plane.

You feel the energy culminate and whoosh out of your body, but without the accompanying euphoria or physical ecstasy of orgasm. You may shake, you may tremble, you may break out into a sweat. Congratulations, you've learned to use your body to tap into the spiritual realm.

Some might call this experience the gold standard, and they wouldn't be wrong. But be patient because it doesn't happen every time and can take a while to master. Start your Karezza sex journey aiming for both partners to feel connected, loved, and satisfied. Powerfully mind-blowing exchanges will come with awareness, experience, and time.

Pro Tip: These spiritual climaxes require high sexual energy and a deep connection. Therefore, the longer your retention streak and stronger your daily Karezza sex habit, the more likely they are to happen.

HOW A GENTLEMAN FINISHES KAREZZA SEX

Sometimes following an energetic exchange, you collapse into each other's arms and both know - it's over. But many times you'll reach that stage... yet you both

136

want to ride the bliss wave for a while. Nothing wrong with that. After all, there are few better ways to pass an evening than with your penis inside a vagina.

In terms of how and when to wrap things up, that's usually up to the man as the leader in the sexual dance. As a gentleman, the first thing you want to keep in mind is whether you're both satisfied.

With practice, you should be able to tell if she feels properly energized, but until then don't be afraid to say something like *'Are you feeling good? Are you feeling satisfied or would you like some more?'* See how she responds and maintain your strong, caring, leadership mindset. If she wants or needs more, a gentleman is always more than happy to oblige.

WHEN TO CUT IT SHORT

Occasionally, you may need to cut Karezza sex short before you're both fully energized and satisfied. That's okay. Since Karezza sex is journey-focused, finishing is more of a pause than a true ending. An interruption of a couple hours or even days won't irritate you like it would if you had cut orgasm-sex short.

One reason to cut Karezza sex short is if you're having trouble holding your nut. Perhaps you've slowed down and cooled off a few times, but the urge to bust keeps returning. Time to call it a night. Explain to your woman she's so sexy tonight you can barely hold back your sperm.

She may say something like *"why not just go ahead and do it?"* Many well-meaning women will suggest this -

especially early on in the Karezza sex journey before the benefits and routine have become firmly established.

Reiterate to her you want to become the greatest version of yourself and the man she deserves. When you're close to the edge, even remaining stationary inside her can be dangerous. Gently pull out and kiss her all over. Make a loving promise to each other to resume as soon as possible.

Also, encourage your woman to let you know if *she* gets close to orgasm. During different phases of her menstrual cycle (especially near ovulation) she may be prone to overstimulation. The better she becomes at speaking up, the better partner you can be in helping her avoid orgasm. If she is having trouble retaining on a particular evening, follow the protocol above and know when to pull back, slow down, and adjourn if necessary.

Another reason to cut Karezza sex short is if your woman gets sore. Most women are unaccustomed to quite so many hours of intercourse as you'll be generously delivering on a near-daily basis. Be aware of this and be willing to forfeit longer sessions in the short term for long term gains. Even mass amounts of gentle sex can be a lot for a woman if she's used to typical 5-10 minute sex. The larger your penis is in proportion to her vagina, the more of an issue this can become.

Look for signs she could be uncomfortable and establish an open dialogue around this topic. Women don't want to be responsible for shutting down the fun early - so don't make her feel that way. Gush about what an amazing vagina she has, how you want to take good care of it, and how fun it will be to work up to longer sessions together. A gentleman respects his woman and keeps in mind she's the vulnerable one here - giving you her body to tend to, enjoy, and hopefully treasure.

One final reason to cut Karezza sex short is if your woman just isn't into it for some reason. This is something you might not even notice during orgasm-sex. Karezza sex is so connected that every once in a while you may pick up on some "off" energy from your woman. If this happens, don't put her on the spot but wind it down and focus your time together on talking instead.

As men, we communicate more with our actions. Women need words. Sometimes they just need to talk. A gentleman should be aware of this and lend his ear when required. Ask her what's up. If you have an inkling about something that's upsetting her, steer the conversation in that direction. It can take some linguistic fishing to figure out what's bothering a woman, but the resulting conversation is worthwhile because it will deepen your connection. *Pro Tip:* many times after talking it out, she'll suddenly be in the mood for Karezza sex.

AFTER THE DEED

When traditional sex ends, you feel spent. Unless you were trying to conceive a child, your subconscious realizes you just wasted a great and valuable resource - your sexual energy. There's a deep-seated, innate shame and regret that comes along with that no matter how sexually liberated you consider yourself to be.

What do lovers do after orgasm? They bask in the 'afterglow' which is actually code for they enjoy a few minutes of relief before regret and anxiety kick in. Two addicts, addicted to the world's most pleasurable but shortest acting drug.

They may lay in each other's arms or go to sleep cuddling. But there's a sense of clinging to each other - riding out feelings of confusion and regret together. Commiserating.

If you guessed the feeling after Karezza sex is completely the opposite, congratulations - you're on track to be a Karezza sex master in no time.

After Karezza sex you feel energized. Sure, if it's late at night you may fall asleep in each other's arms. You'll feel very attracted to each other, but not clingy. It can even feel completely natural after Karezza sex to give each other a kiss, hop up out of bed and get right back to pursuing your other priorities and goals.

Karezza sex contributes to your overall success rather than detracting from it. Feeling fully charged? Great, get to work and be creative. Pursue your passion. Take that energy and channel it toward your higher purpose. You won't miss 'afterglow' when you've got the 24/7 Karezza glow. And it never fades - it just keeps getting brighter and brighter.

CHAPTER 9:
KAREZZA QUICKIES: STEP BY STEP GUIDE TO A SHORTER SESSION

Occasionally, you and your woman may want the rejuvenating benefits of Karezza sex but you don't have time for a long session. Fair enough. You should carve out ample time for Karezza sex - but it shouldn't take up more time than you can afford.

But how do you reap the benefits of slow, relaxed energetic exchange when you've only got 5 or 10 minutes to connect? This chapter will give you a step by step approach to get in, get the job done, get out, and get on with whatever else is on your radar.

STEP 1: GET IN

If you're a good leader, maintain a harmonious relationship, and have near-daily Karezza sex with your woman, getting in shouldn't be a problem. When selling your woman on a Karezza quickie, make it personal. Instead of *"we both really need Karezza sex right now"* try something like *"I really need YOU right now. I need your beauty, your spirit, your body, your sexual energy. I need all of you right now. And I need to give you my sexual energy, I need to put myself inside you and show you how I feel about you and how much I want to connect with you."*

She should be putty in your hands when she realizes you're serious. Some women might also respond well to more demanding language. *"I need you to go into the bedroom with me immediately. We're going to take off all our clothes and do exactly what needs to be done. We don't have any choice. I need to bathe in your juices right now and I know you want that even more than I do - so let's go put yin and yang together for the sake of nature and the universe."*

The idea here is to create a playful yet serious sense of urgency and a sense that only she can save the day with her pussy. If you're sincere and respectful but also playful and firm, your Karezza girl will nearly always rise to the occasion of a short-notice Karezza quickie.

STEP 2: GET THE JOB DONE

In open-ended Karezza sex, the goal is full energy exchange. For a Karezza quickie, a good goal is to make a deep, meaningful connection with your partner. This simple, realistic aim takes the pressure off. You might not create mind-bending sexual poetry when you barely have time to get warmed up. But you *can* create a meaningful interaction that deepens and enriches your relationship and your day - and makes you both feel great.

A relationship is a game of inches, not yards. Every bit of connection, every bit of sweetness counts. What we do every day matters. This is the rationale behind the

Karezza quickie: that a brief, meaningful, loving encounter can be better than putting sex off until more time is available.

One thing to avoid during a Karezza quickie is any tendency toward more lustful, visual, surface-level sex. Stick with your regular Karezza techniques and your calm, patient, masculine mindset. Connect with your woman. Tell her how much you appreciate being with her even if it's just for a few minutes. Tell her how much it energizes you. Ask her if she feels the same way.

Tell her how beautiful she is, how amazing her body is, how much you love being close and in sync with her. This level of verbal communication makes the experience doubly rewarding to your woman, which in turn makes her more apt to do it again.

STEP 3: GET OUT

Getting out of a Karezza quickie is harder than it sounds. You probably won't want to take it out. One fun way to tackle this situation is to go ahead and 'end' the session with a few minutes still left on the clock. Then, go back in for encores. Women love this. The idea that she's so magnetic you had to have just another minute inside her will drive her crazy with love and happiness.

She will fall in love with you all over again when you do this. Men who only practice orgasm-sex have no idea this is even possible because when they're done, they're *done*. No going back in for a sexy encore. Score yet another advantage for Karezza sex.

STEP 4: GET ON WITH IT

Sex energizes us. Orgasm depletes us. Yet 99.99% of people believe sex should lead to orgasm. Imagine you and your woman have ten extra minutes available one morning before work.

In one scenario, you have quick orgasm-sex. Afterward, you each go out into the world depleted before the day's real challenges have even arisen. You feel anxious and spent. Duped yet again by the promise of a pleasure so fleeting it's almost comical. You feel like another loser in a world full of losers who willingly accept this losing way of life.

Now consider a different scenario. This time, you spend your ten minutes on a Karezza quickie. Afterward, you go out into the world full of energy, a fire in your belly, a song in your heart, a smile on your face, dreams in your head, a goddamn spring in your step.

Starting the day with a traditional quickie is setting yourself up for failure. Taking time during a hectic morning, afternoon, or evening for a Karezza quickie is setting yourself up for success.

Whatever goals you must tackle, a Karezza quickie can inspire you to get the job done. Sometimes a few minutes at the quick charge station is exactly the amount of juice you need.

LONG LIVE THE KAREZZA QUICKIE

Some might scoff at the idea of a Karezza quickie. That isn't how it's done, they say. Don't listen to them. If you have a strong connection with your woman, you'll both want sex nearly every day or night. But you may both be extremely driven toward your purpose in life, you may have many responsibilities, you may have kids. Maybe you're working toward a more flexible schedule but you're not there yet.

Karezza sex should not be reserved solely for the leisure class who can afford to invest multiple hours every night into the perfect sexual encounter. Karezza sex must also be available to the go-getters, the hustlers, the hanging-on-by-a-thread-but-getting-the-job-doners, the dog-tired-but-gonna-make-today-count-and-connect-with-my-woman-for-a-few-minutes-before-we-both-pass-out-from-exhaustioners.

Don't let anyone tell you how you can or cannot have sex. A quickie is not the ultimate form of Karezza sex. It's not a substitute for longer sessions. But you'll have plenty of those. You will naturally prioritize time together and fit in multiple longer sessions per week. But when time is very tight, a Karezza quickie may be better for both partners than waiting for the perfect opportunity. Long live the Karezza quickie!

CHAPTER 10:
KAREZZA SEX & YOUR BALLS & YOUR PROSTATE & YOUR COCK

If you've read this far, you're likely sold on the benefits of Karezza sex. As a life hack, it's unrivaled. But what about your prostate, balls, and cock? Is Karezza good for your sex organs? From blue balls to prostate cancer, there are legitimate concerns. For answers, we turn to science.

KAREZZA SEX AND YOUR BALLS

If there's one thing you don't want to risk fucking with, it's your balls. This is your DNA code. The future of your family tree you happen to carry around in a nutsack between your legs. The hormonal source of your testosterone and manliness. You know why it hurts so badly to get hit in the nuts? *Because they're so important.*

BLUE BALLS

Balls produce sperm and testosterone. If they break, you won't feel manly anymore or become a daddy. Your nuts are crucial. We've all heard the term *blue balls*. Epididymal hypertension is the scientific term for blue balls - pain in your testicles from a long erection with no release. Blue balls are caused by excessive blood flow to your nutsack which causes your balls to ache temporarily from built up pressure.

Blue balls is not a serious condition. It can be relieved by orgasm. but it is just as effectively relieved by becoming unaroused. That's not opinion, it's in the official medical literature. When your arousal fully dissipates, your blue balls fade away.

Karezza gentlemen don't report many issues with blue balls. It's not 100% known why. It's possible Karezza sex trains your balls to behave differently, more accustomed to longer, stronger boners and able to handle the blood flow efficiently without aching. Some guys report occasional aching in one or both nuts but nothing major. Rest or a cold shower usually does the trick. Most longtime enthusiasts report having zero issues whatsoever.

EPIDIDYMITIS

The other major issue when discussing testicular health is epididymitis. Epididymitis is inflammation of the pathway between your balls and your dick. It's a serious condition that can lead to sterility in extreme cases. Epididymitis is caused by outside bacteria. This type of bacteria would typically be flushed out during ejaculation, but if it sits in that pathway too long it can cause epididymitis.

Masturbatory edging has a reputation for causing epididymitis. However, there's a key difference between edging and Karezza sex. Masturbatory edging involves your hands, which contain lots of bacteria picked up throughout the day. Most guys don't exactly scrub their hands squeaky clean before jerking off. Guys with their shit together at that level probably don't masturbate.

Also, during edging you abuse your balls and the epididymal pathway by allowing your sperm to flow all the way to the very edge before denying yourself release. It's easy to imagine how a long edging session and some dirty hands could lead to painful inflammation down there.

Karezza sex is very different from masturbatory edging. Karezza sex isn't about teasing your vital fluids to the point of release then stopping at the last second. That's unnatural. Karezza sex is natural. Done skillfully, Karezza sex engages your penis but not your balls.

Keep it clean and you won't have anything to worry about. Put your clean penis in clean pussy, stay well washed, wear clean underwear, don't play with yourself. Your body fights off all kinds of bacteria every day without mechanical flushing. If you follow these guidelines your testicles will stay largely bacteria free so lack of ejaculation won't be an issue.

One of the many great things about having a pair of balls is if there's a problem down there, you'll know it. There's no pain quite like testicular pain. With Karezza sex, recurring or severe nut pain is unlikely. If it occurs, go see a doc, get an antibiotic, and you'll be fine.

KAREZZA SEX AND YOUR PROSTATE

Your prostate is an internal gland between your balls and your ass. It creates the semen that's later mixed with sperm from your balls prior to ejaculation. You may have heard the claim that ejaculation prevents prostate cancer. This claim is often used to justify masturbation. The flip side inference is that not ejaculating could raise your risk of prostate cancer. As far as actual science goes, neither of those statements is accurate.

THE SCIENTIFIC STUDIES

There were two studies a while back that linked ejaculation frequency at various points in a man's life with his risk for prostate cancer later on. One study found that some men who ejaculated almost daily in young adulthood had a lower risk of prostate cancer later in life, when compared to men who ejaculated 2-3 times per week during young adulthood. Another study found that men who ejaculated almost daily later in life had a lower risk of prostate cancer than men who ejaculated only a couple times per week.

It should be noted that these studies included no data on men who didn't ejaculate at all (or very rarely). The studies also did not establish causation, only that the two variables appeared to occur simultaneously. This is not to make light of the correlation they found - it was statistically significant. However, other studies attempting to duplicate these findings have failed to produce a similar correlation.

CORRELATION VS. CAUSATION

What could be the cause of the correlations in these studies? It could be that ejaculating sporadically 2-3 times a week stops and starts your prostate in a way that causes inflammation and is potentially carcinogenic. If that's the case, then ejaculating rarely or never during Karezza sex would offer the same protective benefits as doing it almost daily.

A second possibility is that men who ejaculated more frequently also had more sex, which is known to produce many positive health and lifestyle benefits that could lower your overall cancer risk. If that's the case then Karezza sex surely produces the same benefits, without the drawbacks of orgasm.

A third possibility is that men who ejaculated 2-3 times a week experienced tremendous mood swings between orgasms which drove them to other unhealthy habits that increase cancer rates: overeating, drinking, smoking, drugs, and sedentary lifestyle.

A fourth possibility is that the men who ejaculated every day lowered their testosterone and growth hormone to unnatural and sub-optimal levels. Scientists have established a link between excessively high IGF-1 (insulin-like growth factor hormone) levels and prostate cancer. Ejaculation lowers testosterone, which lowers IGF-1. Daily ejaculation could potentially lower IGF-1 to unnaturally low levels. It is conceivable that excessively low IGF-1 levels could reduce your risk of prostate cancer to lower than average.

However, lowering your IGF-1 to unnaturally low levels is not a healthy way to reduce your risk of cancer. Symptoms of low IGF-1 include anxiety, depression, fatigue, feelings of isolation, and loss of muscle mass. This is essentially the description of someone who ejaculates too much.

If IGF-1 depletion is how the daily ejaculators cut their prostate cancer risk, you can find a better preventative than living out the hellish plight of the daily jizzer. Remember, neither of the studies took into account whether the daily ejaculators had a higher incidence of other diseases and early mortality brought on by their habitual life force depletion.

All this is to point out that these studies were far from scientifically conclusive. The causes could be many. When you consider all the health benefits associated with Karezza sex and a strong relationship plus all the good health habits that come along with strengthening your delayed-gratification muscle, it's hard not to imagine that Karezza sex likely boosts your overall health and lifespan.

PROSTATE CANCER: WHAT SCIENCE SAYS

One in nine men will be diagnosed with prostate cancer in his lifetime. One in 41 men will die of this serious disease, but it is also highly treatable. With regular checkups and health monitoring, it is usually caught early. In terms of risk, age plays the largest role, along with family history and African heritage.

Some have speculated that since black men have both higher rates of prostate cancer and up to 20% higher

152

average testosterone levels compared to the overall population, testosterone could be a culprit. Does testosterone cause prostate cancer?

Regarding testosterone and prostate cancer, here's what we know. There are two types of prostate cancer: a non-aggressive, easy-to-treat form and an aggressive form that is difficult to treat and often deadly. Scientists have found high testosterone levels may raise the risk of the easy-to-treat type, but also *lower* the risk of the aggressive type of prostate cancer.

Current theories on the cause of prostate cancer attribute it to a mix of genetic factors, your prostate's oxidant/antioxidant balance, and complex vitamin, mineral, and hormonal interactions in your body. Preventative measures include the antioxidants selenium, Vitamin E, and lycopene, all of which have solid science behind them.

THE PSA TEST CONTROVERSY

When discussing prostate cancer it's also worth noting that the scientist who first discovered PSA (prostate specific antigen, the blood test for prostate cancer) claims the test is misused and produces false positives in the majority of cases.

This is not to say that prostate cancer isn't serious, but Dr. Richard J. Ablin, the inventor of the PSA test points out that many unnecessary but profitable surgeries are performed on men who score badly on the PSA test but whose cancer cells are unlikely to ever become aggressive or spread.

Ablin and many physicians suggest that close monitoring is often a better approach than radical surgery, but the majority of doctors may not want to risk a lawsuit by recommending a less aggressive option.

YOUR PROSTATE: THE BOTTOM LINE

Now you know the good, the bad, and the ugly when it comes to your prostate. The bottom line is there's never been a study linking not ejaculating to prostate cancer. Skillful, controlled Karezza sex doesn't engage your prostate (or balls) much in the first place.

The deeper story is that the Karezza sex lifestyle improves health and well-being in so many ways that a healthier, longer lifespan is the only logical result of Karezza sex.

If you're concerned about prostate cancer, good. It's something all men should be aware of. The best approach is to take selenium, Vitamin E, and lycopene, and to maintain good overall health and fitness. There is also some evidence that limiting dairy consumption may reduce risk. See your doctor regularly and get tested when appropriate.

Prostate cancer is dangerous but so is being overcautious and getting spooked by half-baked science just because a lot of guys quote it to justify their orgasm addiction.

Karezza enthusiasts are pioneers. Pioneering always requires taking calculated risks with real life consequences. Taking calculated risks is what separates the men from the boys and the one percent from the ninety-nine.

Karezza gentlemen are rational thinkers. Possible (but not probable) slightly elevated risk of a highly treatable disease in exchange for all the riches and joys of Karezza sex? If this sounds like an acceptable risk to you then congratulations, you have a sharp intellect and the balls to try something different. You're going to absolutely love Karezza sex.

KAREZZA SEX AND YOUR COCK

As men, we don't want to hurt our penises. Many of us remember adolescent years of roughing the poor fellow up so badly it was literally self-abuse. Whether or not that was you, you might want some assurance the massive amounts of Karezza sex you're about to engage in won't put too much wear and tear on your manhood.

Nothing to worry about. There is probably no limit to the amount of Karezza sex you can safely and happily pursue with your partner. Slow, mindful sex in a wet, juicy pussy - what could go wrong?

If you follow the tips in this book, your woman will create plenty of natural lubrication. And since the sex will be more controlled and less acrobatic, there's virtually no risk of penile fractures which can occur during fast, lustful orgasm-sex.

So long as you are with your trusted partner who is free of sexually transmitted diseases, your penis should be 100% safe during the massive amounts of Karezza sex you'll be having. In fact, your penis will actually benefit greatly from Karezza sex in at least a couple ways.

First, Karezza sex will make your cock stronger. The penis is in many ways like a muscle: the more you use it, the stronger and mightier it gets. Spending so much time having sex also helps you develop mind-penis connectivity - once you unlock this awareness it instantly makes you a better lover.

Second, the skin on your penis will benefit from the soothing moisture of Jing Juice. What better moisturizer for your most primal organ than nature's own lubricant - the same fluids that warmly usher a new baby into the world? Yes, Karezza sex is great for your cock.

KAREZZA SEX AS NATURE'S PLAN FOR MEN

Our potential for sexual transmutation is no accident. It's also built into many of our animal cousins who mate according to the strict rhythms of nature and at all other times channel their sexual energy into dominance and survival.

What if our bodies are naturally designed for Karezza sex and the majority who indulge in non-procreative orgasm are abusing their reproductive systems - putting their fertility and health at risk?

As human males, we are not subject to strict mating seasons like animals or the pull of the moon on our bodies like women. We must create our own sexual habits and rhythms and live or die by them. Given its health, financial, relationship, productivity, and happiness benefits, Karezza sex seems to be rewarded by the universe. This strongly suggests it's the correct use of one's sexual energy. If that's the case, perhaps nature made provisions to protect your balls and prostate.

One of the top benefits of Karezza sex is that it inspires you to take care of your health. Exercise, eat right, take vitamins, see the doctor regularly and most importantly educate yourself on your body, health, nutrition, and fitness. If any problems ever do arise, you'll be aware and on top of them.

Reminder: This book is not intended as a substitute for professional medical advice. You should regularly consult a health professional, particularly with respect to any symptoms that may require diagnosis or medical attention.

CHAPTER 11:
DOWN N' DIRTY KAREZZA Q & A

Condoms, Kink, Polyamory, Escorts, Exhibitionism, Alcohol, Weed, Menstruation, Porn, Masturbation, etc. The purpose of this book is to cover every situation a man might encounter on his Karezza sex journey, so it's time to get down and dirty with real talk and solid advice on some controversial topics.

CONDOMS AND KAREZZA SEX?

Condoms are not ideal for Karezza sex, however there are times they might be in everyone's best interest. Condoms put a latex barrier between your penis and her vagina. This can mute the flow of sexual energy. On the other hand, there aren't any great birth control options for women. The hormonal methods wreak havoc on their natural hormone balance. The mechanical methods such as IUDs are risky and barbaric. But pregnancy is also a risk, so use condoms if you must while you master your sense of your control.

Once you've established trust, discussed STDs, and tamed your ejaculatory reflex, a good next step is to dispense with the condoms and go in raw. Just make sure you pull out any time you feel close to even pre-ejaculation. This keeps you from breaking your retention streak and also prevents pregnancy. For another layer of protection, there are apps for a woman to track her cycle and most fertile days (there are only a few every month). You can be extra careful on those days.

The good news about starting Karezza sex with a condom is it can dull your sensitivity just enough to help you get started with orgasm control. You might even say condoms are the 'training wheels' of Karezza sex.

Conversely, when you stop using condoms, be aware that you'll suddenly be *more* sensitive, so you may need to work harder to avoid orgasm. By that time, you'll have the skills, confidence, and control to do so.

KINK AND KAREZZA SEX?

Kink is defined as "a person's unusual sexual preference." Sounds harmless enough. We all have different affinities. The question is whether your kink enhances your connection or distracts from it. Being honest about your unique preferences can enhance your connection. But when kink becomes the focus, something deeper is lost.

If your kink is an affinity for a body part like feet there should be plenty of opportunity to incorporate some foot rubbing or toe licking into Karezza sex.

If your kink is role play, try it in a positive way that affirms your relationship rather than subverting it. Play the roles of a favorite fictional couple whose relationship you admire or become your own best future selves. Be creative and use the elements that feel right to you. Karezza sex is about being present, not escaping.

Your girl likes being tied up? Try holding her hands up behind her head, fingers entwined, lovingly restraining her as you unapologetically exert dominion over her lower half. She'll feel overpowered but in a natural and beautiful way.

If your kink is something painful, humiliating, or abusive, it's likely a bad fit. Karezza sex is open to interpretation and experimentation, but it's also based on a loving, gentle vibe. Karezza sex is not about the nasty side of life - it's a sanctuary from that. It's the best of what sex can be - not the ugliest or most extreme.

Karezza sex is about integrating your sexual energy into one congruent existence in and out of the bedroom. Kink is often about compartmentalizing your sexual energy and personality. Kink play tends to be thrill oriented and geared toward letting off excess sexual energy that needs an outlet. Interestingly, our wildest sexual impulses often translate most readily to genius when rechanneled into transmutation. Letting off steam may feel healthy in the short run, but transmutation feels divine.

POLYAMORY AND KAREZZA SEX?

If sex with one woman is great, two must be better. It's hard to argue with that logic. In the realm of orgasm-sex, the math surely seems to add up. Might not make for the most fulfilling relationship but double the pussy must be *at least* double the fun, right? And if two is great, what about three? Maybe a whole harem. After all, monogamy is outdated and oppressive.

Maybe you're even willing to allow your woman equal freedom. Then you can swap partners with other couples - a constant supply of fresh pussy. So long as you're cool with handing your woman over to other men in exchange for fucking their women.

Maybe you're a throuple, or maybe there are five or ten of you who all live together and sleep and fuck in one big bed. It may be a great lifestyle for some people, but for others it's largely cheap thrills. The thrill of the variety, the thrill of breaking taboos, the thrill of exhibitionism and voyeurism. It will be very hard to hold back your jizz when you have a constant supply of fresh females opening themselves up to you.

As humans we have a built in need to be somebody's *everything*. This need can lead to pain and heartache but that doesn't mean it's unhealthy. It's built into who we are, just like the drive to dominate and succeed is built into men and can also lead to pain and heartache.

Polyamory may be satisfying on powerful levels. But deep down you may be sacrificing a basic human need for something more novel, thrilling, and exciting but ultimately less fulfilling.

Through Karezza sex, you become aware of sexual energy in every situation. You might feel a deep need to exchange energy with a variety of different people, but never realized you can do so through higher chakras and non-sexual forms of expression. Once you learn this, the urge for multiple sex partners may seem like overkill.

There are many types of people in the world. Polyamory might be a solid option for some. But in terms of building a sustainable future, one solid woman at a time has many benefits. The most obvious benefit is that monogamy frees up the rest of your sexual energy - and time and money - for achievement and advancement. That's what transmutation is all about. It's hard to get much work done with unlimited sex partners. It's hard to keep from jizzing all over the place, too. And without retention, there is no Karezza sex.

ESCORTS AND KAREZZA SEX?

Prostitution is often called the world's oldest profession. What's between a woman's legs has always been highly prized by men. We pay for it one way or another, the thinking goes, so why not just pay upfront? There are many fascinating moral arguments for and against prostitution. But if you're reading this book, you're man enough to decide for yourself if paying a stranger for sex fits into your moral framework and moves you forward in an authentic and sustainable way.

Aside from the moral grey zone, another thing to be concerned about with prostitutes is disease. Condoms only protect against so much. If you're health conscious it's hard to justify close bodily contact with the germs of a prostitute *and* every man she's been with. Another issue to be aware of is that many prostitutes are owned and exploited by pimps and traffickers.

Paying for sex could also become addictive because it imbues you with the scarcity-mindset belief that you *can't* get sex without paying for it.

As for practicing Karezza sex with a prostitute - do you really want to make out with and slow-bang a prostitute in an intimate embrace for two hours? Why not find and turn a real woman into your Karezza girl? With a girlfriend you can do it every night. That's a lot more bang for your buck.

The point of Karezza sex is: the best sex is controlled, connected, loving sex. Sex where you give your heart to your woman along with your penis. Can you give your heart to a prostitute during a sexual encounter? If you do, how will you feel afterward when your time is up and she's onto her next client? Sounds like a good way to go broke.

Lonely men may see prostitutes as a good stepping stone toward a girlfriend. She won't judge their inexperience and doesn't want anything in return except cash. For certain guys it could be a viable option. But if you feel you must hire a prostitute, at least treat her with respect. She already knows she's a whore and probably wishes she weren't. Make your encounter one that lifts her up and encourages her in some way. Give her some good energy. Treat her as well as you would any other woman who opened herself up and made herself vulnerable to you.

EXHIBITIONISM AND KAREZZA SEX?

The desire to show off our sexual energy, to make many people see it, feel it, be impacted by it. This desire is the root of genius and drive. Exhibitionism is a fruitless manifestation of this healthy desire.

Exhibitionism, such as making sex videos and posting them online, or livestreaming your encounters, can feel exhilarating and healthy. It fulfills our core desire to be seen and make an impact. It also feels very sex-positive and sex is inarguably a great thing.

The problem with exhibitionism is that you allow your sexual energy to manifest in its lowest and most basic form - raw sexual exposure - instead of channeling it toward greatness. By resisting the exhibitionist urge, you force your energy to manifest at higher levels. This is the source of creativity, the arts, invention, and ingenuity.

The other problem with exhibitionism is its effect on the viewer. Maybe you create a beautiful video of you and your woman having sweet Karezza sex for two hours. This may indeed be useful and educational. But that's not how it will be used by most who see it - they'll just jerk off to it like any other porn.

As an exhibitionist you become a purveyor of porn and titillation. That's tricky moral territory. It's one thing to take the sexual low-road yourself, but to tempt and lead others down that road comes with some funky karma. There are many richer, cleaner, and more profitable ways to make an impact and show the world what you're made of.

ALCOHOL AND KAREZZA SEX?

Many people use alcohol to relax and unwind, sometimes leading to sex. However, alcohol dulls awareness and the senses. Alcohol prevents appreciation of subtle nuances in energy. For these reasons, alcohol is not ideal for Karezza sex. Rely instead on the closeness and intimacy of your connection for that feeling of calm and relaxation and you won't need it.

Alcohol can also lead to the impulsive decision to orgasm. Alcohol makes you passive and less masculine, less hard. Your dick may be hard but your attitude isn't. You can't channel pure masculine energy if you're adulterating it with alcohol first.

Alcohol may help prevent premature ejaculation in some cases, but overall it's not the best strategy. Alcohol isn't particularly beneficial to long term health, spiritual growth, or sexual energy awareness.

Sometimes a drink may be on the menu and that's no reason to skip sex. But as a general rule, drown your anxiety in action, not booze.

WEED AND KAREZZA SEX?

Marijuana has been used as an aphrodisiac for thousands of years. It's known to enhance the sexual experience. Weed can make you feel sexier, more aware, more polarized. It can allow you to experience the deeper levels and meaning of Karezza sex quicker than you might otherwise.

Of course, every benefit comes with a cost. The most obvious cost of using weed in your Karezza practice is your connection with your partner. Skillful and deep Karezza sex invokes the duality of connectedness and polarity. To achieve full connectedness, you and your partner must be on the same wavelength. To achieve perfect exchange of sexual energy your minds must connect as well as your bodies and spirits. Weed can obfuscate the mental part of this connection.

You can have great Karezza sex on weed, but it may be more beneficial in the long run to put in the work to get there naturally. Weed can be a solid awareness tool for some people, but if it's the only way you can have great Karezza sex, curb your use until that's no longer the case.

PREMATURE EJACULATION AND KAREZZA SEX?

Many men find it difficult to hold their nut even during regular sex. If I can't last 2 minutes, these men wonder, how can I last an hour or more? The key is mindset training. Here are a few tips

First, stop thinking of yourself as a man who suffers from premature ejaculation. Premature ejaculation may be something that's happened to you in the past, but it's not your identity or an immutable characteristic. Shed the label and move on.

Next, remember a key difference: during traditional sex, one of the primary goals is ultimately ejaculation. You might say that men who ejaculate prematurely are overly in tune with that goal.

During Karezza sex, you're not heading toward ejaculation at all. Since ejaculation is not the goal, your brain has a much easier task. Rather than trying to distract yourself and pretend ejaculation isn't the goal when it actually is, you can devote your entire awareness to avoiding ejaculation altogether. This is a game changer.

In fact, Karezza sex gives a man all the tools he needs to conquer premature ejaculation once and for all. The rhythm is slower and more mindful. Your awareness is on sexual energy rather than body parts. Your focus is on transmutation rather than orgasm. It's a whole new way of relating to sex.

ANORGASMIA VS. KAREZZA SEX?

Certain medications, especially SSRI antidepressants, cause a condition called anorgasmia. Anorgasmia is defined as a "inability to achieve orgasm despite responding to sexual stimulation." Yes, if you pop certain pills you can have relatively decent sex without any possibility of orgasm.

But it's nothing like Karezza sex. The reason is that anorgasmia results from lack of ability to tap into your full sexual energy. You're so blissed-out on meds you can't summon up the wherewithal to cum.

Karezza transmutation absolutely requires you to tap fully into your raw sexual energy, and learn to master it. While anorgasmia and Karezza sex might look similar on the surface, the similarities end there. They don't feel the same and the results are not the same.

MENSTRUATION AND KAREZZA SEX?

One tricky aspect of any relationship is a woman's monthly menstrual period. Just when the energy is flowing perfectly... an interruption. And it happens every four weeks. Even though it comes around like clockwork, many men still find it jarring to suddenly be cut off from sex for a few days. It can cause relationship discord if not managed properly.

One increasingly popular solution to this pickle is to have sex during menstruation. Google 'sex during menstruation' and the top results are mostly purported benefits. One site touts saving money on lube as a benefit. Use blood instead, they recommend. Another site recommends menstrual sex because it's more 'exciting'. Other sites claim period sex cures menstrual cramps and headaches.

The other option is to abstain from intercourse during your woman's period. Throughout history, many major traditions have advocated this. From a relationship standpoint, taking a break shows respect for your woman's body which is attempting to pass uterine tissue and blood. In a literal sense, menstrual sex goes against the flow of nature.

Pausing sex for menstruation also demonstrates to your woman that you're not addicted to her pussy. It shows you're perfectly happy to transmute your energy into higher pursuits when sex is not available. This fortifies your leadership status in the relationship. Undertaken with a gratitude mindset, a monthly abstinence period is excellent transmutation practice for both partners. It's also a good opportunity to cultivate other aspects of your connection.

Karezza couples have it easier than most during a menstrual pause since they aren't addicted to orgasm. Yes, a few days without sex can be unpleasant when you're used to heavenly Karezza sex nightly. If your sexual energy is strong, it can legitimately feel excruciating. But that's nothing compared to the pain of orgasm withdrawal.

Karezza sex brings you into flow with nature. With practice, taking a short monthly pause during menstruation can become a valued and welcome part of the flow. If you find the monthly break from intimacy damages your relationship, try naked make out and fondling sessions to keep the intimacy and sexual energy flowing.

PORN AND KAREZZA SEX?

Porn is widely accepted as harmless fun. It's become ubiquitous in today's world. The line between porn and non-porn is constantly eroding. Porn is big business. The people who produce and sell it are similar to drug dealers: they know the power of their product and their goal is to get you hooked and make you helpless.

Porn turns you into a spectator. Your mindset becomes *they do it, I watch.* Since your sexual energy is the root of your life energy, that spectator mindset extends to other areas of life too. *They do it, I watch.* This is the destructive subconscious mantra of porn-addicted men everywhere.

Porn use also makes it difficult to retain your seed and avoid orgasm. Your subconscious doesn't realize you're looking at a computer or phone screen. All it sees is tons of people fucking and jizzing all over the place. The world must be ending, it assumes. *These people are going at it so hard it must be the last chance to procreate before some cataclysmic event.*

Your subconscious then decides that busting a nut is a top priority and it will make you hornier and hornier until that's exactly what you do. We like to think we can overpower instinct with reason, but our eyes see everybody fucking like wild animals and our subconscious figures we'd better get in on that. If you watch porn, holding your nut long term will become torturous to the point it's counterproductive.

There are other reasons to avoid porn in a relationship, too. No matter how sexy your woman is she can only be one type. If she's white, she can't be black, if she's tall, she can't be short, if she has a tight little ass she can't have a fat ass. And she can only be one girl, not two girls, three girls, or more. If you watch porn you will never be satisfied with the woman you have right in your own bed, no matter how great she is. That's a tragedy.

The scenarios in most porn also tend to be immoral or otherwise disturbing: cheating, abuse, incest, rape, humiliation, pain, degradation. This is gutter-level behavior. And the mass majority of today's men consume this depravity on a daily basis.

The good news is once you quit porn, you gain a huge advantage over all the men who can't even look themselves in the mirror and admit the type of sick depraved videos they watch every day.

Stay away from porn in your Karezza relationship and keep your woman away from it too. Practicing Karezza sex in today's world means going against the grain. Quitting porn gives you the mental fortitude to do exactly that. It also makes you a better lover, a stronger man, and a leader worth following.

Pro Tip: Watching your own sex in the mirror can have the same effect as porn, with an added narcissistic element that can become addictive. It heightens the visual aspect of your encounter and takes the focus off your sexual energy. If there's a mirror near where you have Karezza sex, try not to steal more than an occasional glance or two.

MASTURBATION AND KAREZZA SEX?

Karezza sex is about generating sexual energy and channeling it to the highest and best use possible. Masturbation - with or without orgasm - is the lowest form of sexual behavior. It's a futile attempt to exchange sexual energy with yourself. To get high on your own supply. Don't masturbate in a Karezza relationship. It defeats the purpose.

Masturbation leads to anxiety, shame, and mood swings. Not because society has repressed you. Your own subconscious primal programming knows it's wrong because masturbation holds you back from actual success, survival, and reproduction.

Jerking off is not a good way to stoke your sexual energy. It's not a good way to feel energized. It significantly lowers your self-respect and drive. Just because ninety-nine percent of men do it, don't let yourself be dragged down with them.

As a man, masturbation also turns your penis into a passive sexual object - like a vagina - because you're doing something *to* it rather than *with* it. Masturbation also turns you into a man who strokes cock. Yes it happens to be your own cock, but the fact remains you're utilizing your hands not to build something great or do something worthwhile, but to stroke cock. There's something distinctly feminine about that activity that more men should probably be mindful of.

Your woman shouldn't masturbate either. Sex wasn't designed to be enjoyed solo. Masturbation isn't a life hack - it's degeneracy. Karezza sex requires a mindset different from the mass majority. Women's media relentlessly promote masturbation and orgasm as a must for modern women. As the leader in your relationship, make it a priority to teach your woman that masturbation is as poisonous to women as it is to men.

Take charge gently but firmly. Draw an unambiguous line in the sand that there should be no masturbation on either of your parts. This includes when you're in bed together. Touch each other, not yourselves to keep the energy flowing smoothly, happily, and abundantly.

WET DREAMS AND KAREZZA SEX?

You're retaining. You're transmuting. You're loving life. Karezza sex is going beautifully on every level. Then the unthinkable happens. A wet dream. Did you ruin your streak? Will you lose your superpowers? Will your transmutation sputter?

In the midst of a solid retention streak, a nocturnal emission can feel like a gut punch. Betrayed by your own body while you were sleeping. But fear not. Most men report they don't suffer nearly the same setbacks from a wet dream as they do from conscious ejaculation and orgasm.

The best way to recover? Keep retaining and have plenty of Karezza sex. Over time, you'll train your body and your subconscious to separate the emotion of sex from the act of ejaculation. This will lead to less and less frequent nocturnal emissions in the future.

CLITORAL STIMULATION AND KAREZZA SEX?

There's a hot debate among Karezza enthusiasts regarding clitoral stimulation. To some, it's a normal part of their routine. Others believe direct manual stimulation of the clitoris throws sexual energy out of balance. The idea is that too much direct clitoral stimulation puts a woman directly into a lustful, orgasm-chasing state.

Which side is correct? Everybody's different, but it's good to be aware of the concerns about clitoral stimulation. A good rule of thumb for all kinds of stimulation during Karezza sex is: if it gives you or your partner the uncontrollable urge to orgasm, steer away from it and in a direction that feels more sustainable. Vaginal intercourse, body-to-body intimacy (including incidental clitoral stimulation) and nipple stimulation may create a more balanced and loving erotic state.

ORGASMS AND KAREZZA SEX?

There are many flavors of spiritual sex. Most of them involve orgasms: dry orgasms, wet orgasms, multiple orgasms, full body orgasms. You may even hear people suggest you can have orgasms during Karezza sex. You cannot. Unless they are truly accidental.

Karezza sex is connected, loving, mindful, controlled, respectful sex *without orgasm or pursuit of orgasm.* You

174

can have mindful, connected orgasm-sex, but it won't draw you closer and closer over time like the magnetic pull of Karezza sex. It also won't transmute your energy toward genius the way Karezza sex will.

Some Karezza enthusiasts opt for regularly scheduled infrequent orgasms and say that works well for them. Others aim to retain their orgasm as long as possible and master the art of transmutation. The former group get a taste of the benefits while the latter group reap the *full benefits* of Karezza sex.

IS KAREZZA SEX SATISFYING?

Not only is Karezza sex satisfying, it's infinitely more satisfying (in real time and as an overall practice) than orgasm sex. Imagine learning to use your penis in an entirely new way. Not to pee, not to cum, but as a rock steady transmitter and receiver of pure, clean, potent sexual energy. Imagine that the profound pleasure you got from that was not only sexual but existential in nature.

Sexual energy is your most important and consequential energy. Proper channeling of this energy is the recipe for winning in life. There's nothing more satisfying than knowing your sexual practice is serving your goals. Avoiding the loss of potency and drive after an orgasm is also extremely satisfying. Physically, the pleasure is second to none. Imagine the ecstasy of an orgasm but spread out over the entire length of your encounter and throughout your entire body and spirit. Yes, Karezza sex is extremely satisfying.

WILL KAREZZA SEX RELIEVE MY HORNINESS?

As every man knows, excessive horniness makes it hard to concentrate and get things done. Most men rely on orgasm to relieve that tension and get on with their business. But it's not the only way.

Karezza sex very effectively relieves horniness and sexual tension via transmutation. That's not to say you won't want sex daily. You'll want it more than ever. But it will be a healthy, constructive, controlled desire as opposed to a desperate, needy compulsion.

IS KAREZZA SEX FUN?

Karezza sex isn't merely fun. It's the most fun you can have in bed, period. There's nothing quite as energizing and exciting as confidently wielding your sexual energy in bed to your heart's content. Without the escape and release of orgasm to hide behind, you learn to relax and fully embody your full sexual nature.

The best part is, this ability stays with you 24 hours a day. No longer will you feel like a boy in any situation. You'll always feel like a man. Men who find Karezza sex boring simply aren't doing it right. The key is learning to slow down enough to appreciate the profound beauty of the act.

You want excitement? There's nothing more fun and exciting than exploring a woman's body endlessly and without the distraction of orgasm to get in the way. A dedicated lover of women will never get bored with this.

Not even for a second. Throw in the high level skills you'll develop to avoid orgasm and transmute sexual energy and it all amounts to a nightly naked ritual where the grand prize is all your wildest dreams come true. What could be more fun and exciting than that?

IS KAREZZA SEX HARD?

One of the best things about Karezza sex is it's within reach of every man. We're all sexual by nature. Karezza sex is about stripping away the barriers to that awareness, unleashing your raw energy, and transmuting it in a higher direction. But you need not be a Yogi or a Zen Master to make this happen. All it takes is a familiarity with the principals in this book and some practice.

In fact, any man who reads this book and gives it his best try will succeed. The first few days or weeks there's a learning curve as you detox from orgasm and learn to channel your energy in a new direction. Men who find this overwhelming might abstain from sex while the orgasm addiction subsides (typically 2-4 weeks), then proceed. But this isn't necessary for most men.

If you're in a relationship that relies on sexual intimacy as a key element, taking a month off from sex can have negative ramifications. As an alternative, try slowing down, relaxing, reveling in the intimacy and connectedness, and pausing the action any time you feel yourself veering toward orgasm.

Help your woman through her process as well. Conquering the learning curve together can greatly enhance your relationship and give you a jump start on mastery. The only way to fail at Karezza sex is to quit trying. Don't let accidents or mishaps discourage you. If you persist, you will succeed. And probably much sooner than you expect.

CHAPTER 12:
THE PROCREATIVE URGE

"Reproduction is the fulfillment of divine law."

- Dr. Alice B. Stockham, *Karezza, Ethics of Marriage*

"I call an animal, a species, an individual corrupt when it loses its instincts."

- Friedrich Nietzsche

THE PROCREATIVE URGE

The sexual urge is ultimately the procreative urge and the procreative urge is by design a tyrant. This drive is literally hard-wired into every strand of your DNA. Confronting the procreative urge and integrating it into your awareness can cure much of the anxiety that plagues men today. Ironically, it's the last thing many of us would suspect as the cause of our distress. That's how out of touch we've become with our own nature.

We are animals who live in a physical world. Once we reach full maturity we begin battling against aging and death. It's easy to ignore this glacially slow process, but it dominates our subconscious awareness. This is anxiety.

Currently the only way to physically 'beat' death is to reproduce. Everybody feels this anxiety but we've lost touch with where it comes from, what it means, and most importantly what we can do to alleviate it holistically.

Once you commit to reckoning with your procreative urge, Karezza sex becomes your perfect partner in the process. Karezza sex deepens your relationship, prevents unplanned pregnancy, improves your finances, and sparks personal growth. Karezza sex essentially creates the perfect conditions for successful procreation when you decide the time is right.

In the context of a larger procreative strategy, Karezza sex can be seen as extended foreplay, which may go on for many years. Baby-making sex then becomes the ultimate note of resolution to the Karezza sex symphony. You may not know exactly how or when, but making it one of your concrete life goals to hit that resolution note someday puts the entire symphony into the larger framework of creation of life. The result is music more beautiful than you could ever imagine.

THE WILL TO POWER

19th century German philosopher Friedrich Nietzsche proposed that the fundamental nature of all things in the universe is a "will to power." Will to power can be defined as an insatiable desire to manifest power: to exist, to survive, to improve, to reproduce, to win. Nietzsche cautioned that any morality which requires a man to suppress his will to power is an anti-natural morality that will cause a man to shrivel into nihilism and despair.

One of the biggest messages aimed at young men today is: you should not procreate. *It's too risky. It's unnecessary. It's expensive. It's irresponsible. It's selfish. It will drag you down.* Procreation, the messaging goes, is one of many available lifestyle options. And yet, no mentality could be more damaging to the male psyche. If passing on your unique genes is not important, then you're not important. And if you're not important then what's the point of getting up in the morning?

Anti-natural morality which runs counter to the instincts of life leads to anxiety, depression, addiction, suicide and other modern diseases of despair. Notably, these conditions have risen sharply as our society's fertility rate has dropped like a stone. If you accept that passing your genes along doesn't matter, you're telling yourself, "I hope our species survives, but I'm not man enough to participate. I hope those stronger, more worthy men pass on lots of great genes."

What man can look himself in the mirror with that attitude? Your biological imperative is to go forward regardless. To shirk this drive is what Nietzsche called "losing one's instincts" which he equated with moral corruption. No wonder men today are such a mess.

Of course, procreation may not be every man's calling. Some men are physically unable and some men may feel nobly called toward a purpose that precludes procreation. The point isn't to suggest that such men can't live happy, fulfilling lives. The point is that if you're like most men, it's far more efficient and rewarding to work with your procreative urge rather than fight against it - and that Karezza sex will be your perfect partner in that process.

LONG-DELAYED GRATIFICATION

Sometimes it's easy to forget the *gratification* part of delayed gratification. But our reward pathways are one of our greatest motivators. The goal should not be to shut them off but to rewire yourself (and rearrange your life) so that they serve your highest purpose and drive you forward.

Dopamine isn't the enemy. *Misuse* of dopamine is the enemy. We need dopamine to accomplish our goals. We get a slow drip of dopamine as we work toward our rewards. It's the feeling of anticipation that drives us forward. If you give yourself ridiculously pleasurable rewards for little to no work, you're using dopamine against yourself.

On the other extreme, if you remove the prospect of eventual gratification completely, you may undermine some of dopamine's power to drive you forward. Treating procreative orgasm as the long delayed gratification to your orgasm retention will open your dopamine pathways to function exactly as they were designed. This gives all your efforts an enormous boost.

WOMEN ARE NOT THE PROBLEM

Some men say they don't plan on procreating because women today are 'trash'. The truth is, most people - women and men - go along with the mass majority, which takes its cues from mass media. In the past, the masses were encouraged to be healthy, moral, and to procreate. Now they are encouraged to be selfish, hedonistic consumers. In that sense, most women today are morally adrift. But so are most men.

All it takes for you to find a good woman is to become your best as a man. When you set higher standards for yourself and live up to those standards, women will notice and be drawn to follow you. You won't even have to go looking - the good ones will find you.

Women have always been as difficult as they are delightful. But that's the game. You're here to play it. You beat out billions of other sperm for the chance. Your ancestors sacrificed everything to give you this opportunity. To achieve true fulfillment and peace of mind you must actively flow with nature. Full flow with nature means connecting with a woman. Perfect flow with nature means procreating eventually, if you're physically able.

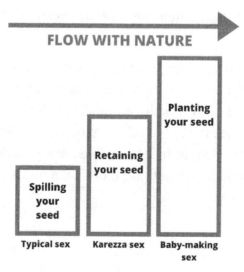

POPULATION IN PERSPECTIVE

Other men have sworn off procreation - to save the world. Humans are nothing but CO2 generators killing the earth, the argument goes. By that logic, how long until people start nobly committing suicide to reduce their carbon footprint? Sounds crazy, but in a sense it's the same mentality.

All organisms are genetically programmed to multiply. No organism tries to shrink its own population. That's a march toward extinction. Genes either proliferate or become extinct.

"Not enough resources to go around" has been a problem since the dawn of life. It's the struggle that defines us. How we solve it defines our future. If there's not enough to go around, we are programmed to fight, to discover, to innovate, to make more. Not to surrender and snuff ourselves out. The earth's getting crowded? Great, let's colonize space. That's risky and will prompt mass casualties? Okay, then we'd better make a shit ton of babies.

There's no other way. Shrinking is not a viable option. Any attempt to override this fundamental code is anti-natural and will result in anxiety, depression, and despair. Eventually total destruction. We see it everywhere. People feel their lives are pointless. They believe humanity is nothing more than a virus infecting a dying planet.

What if you believed instead that you and all of humanity (but especially you) were fucking awesome? What if you were 100% convinced the world needs *more* of you, copies of you, reproductions of you? This is the feeling of being alive. This is embracing your will to power. This is the feeling of running your own show and having the brains and balls to make it happen despite the whole world telling you not to bother.

KAREZZA SUPERBABIES

If Karezza sex feels like heaven, then baby-making sex feels like you're a god. And you *are* a god because you're literally creating another human being with your penis. Karezza lovers have the unique ability to take baby-making sex to the next level.

When the time arrives to conceive, the Karezza gentleman will be so in tune with his woman and so proficient in the art of gentle lovemaking that their conception will be unforgettable - the type of sex only a tiny sliver of humans throughout history have ever experienced.

One can only surmise the resulting offspring could possess an especially pure, strong, noble, and peaceful nature as a result. Does this mean that Karezza sex will produce superbabies? If you follow the energy flow, it's not so far-fetched.

KAREZZA PREGNANCY

Pregnancy is a time when couples should ideally strengthen their bond, but it's actually when many relationships fall apart. Many couples let their closeness disintegrate just when they'll need it more than ever. Lack of sex plus the stress of impending parenthood is a recipe for domestic misery if not properly managed.

Most men are blindsided by this circumstance and fail to take the necessary leadership to maintain intimacy throughout pregnancy. These men fail to prioritize and express their sexual needs and the entire family is worse off for the sexual energy imbalance.

Now imagine the communication toolbox available to a Karezza couple in this situation. A Karezza couple enters into pregnancy with a well-established belief that sex is something beautiful, loving, and caring. They know how to prioritize intimacy. They will figure out ways to interact sexually that are pleasurable, comfortable, positive, and respectful of the woman's body and the growing life inside it. The resulting peace and harmony will benefit the entire family.

KAREZZA PARENTING

A successful procreative strategy requires great parenting. Great parenting first and foremost requires modeling loving and respectful behavior between the father and mother. How you interact with each other becomes your child's model for how to interact with the world. Karezza sex bonds you and your partner, so as parents you have each other's back.

Karezza parents also model more stable emotions and higher self-esteem than their orgasm-addicted counterparts. Karezza sex is the perfect tool for successful parenting. Better focus, energy, money, relationship, patience, creativity, empathy, optimism, and happiness. All the ingredients you need to successfully raise your next generation.

THE KAREZZA DADDY

Fatherhood is a powerful perspective that can lead to boundless personal growth. Of course some very enlightened men never become fathers. But whatever your level of enlightenment before fatherhood - it more than doubles when you become a dad.

Watching your kids grow shows you how you became who you are. Mindful men can harness this insight to grow and change. Most men don't realize this and never take full advantage of the implications, but those who harness this advantage often become unstoppable.

Fatherhood ideally gives you a new urgency to become your best self in order to set an example. Fatherhood also makes you more aggressively willing to take risks. It's not just your own glory on the line anymore - it's your kid's opportunity to eat good food, get a bike, travel, and take advantage of countless other opportunities. Karezza sex gives you all the focus, energy, and creativity you need to fully capitalize on this escalated drive.

THE BIG PICTURE

Most men reading this book probably aren't planning on becoming dads any time soon. Nothing wrong with that. So why include this chapter? Because no book for men on spiritual sex is complete without this discussion.

Not spilling your seed is half the battle. But it's also important to put it where it belongs. If the second part wasn't important, then spilling it wouldn't be such a big deal. Karezza sex in the context of an overall procreative strategy equals getting the most out of sex and living fully in flow with your animal, spiritual, and masculine natures.

CHAPTER 13:
THE KAREZZA GENTLEMAN: A SEXUAL SOLDIER IN A REVOLUTIONARY AGE

"The mass of men live lives of quiet desperation."

- Henry David Thoreau, *Walden*

BLAZE YOUR OWN TRAIL

According to developmental psychologist James Marcia, identity achievement occurs when an individual stakes out his own identity after extensive exploration. This is the opposite of blindly adopting society's values. Marcia cites sex, spirituality, politics, and occupation as the four main aspects of our core identity. Of these four, men seem least apt to chart their own course sexually.

Yes, many men put themselves out there sexually, but leading with your cock doesn't make you a trailblazer. How many men have ever considered the idea of not cumming during sex? It makes perfect sense, and yet most of us never even consider it.

Karezza sex is your opportunity to blaze your own trail. Not just in the bedroom but in your life. Once you break away from the way everyone else has sex, something brilliant occurs. You start doing everything else differently too. Smarter, better. Karezza sex gives you a good-natured superiority complex. *My way is better than yours.* This feeling is addictive - in a good way.

Blazing your own Karezza sex trail gives you the confidence to try many other things your own way too. Your superior mindfulness and energy mean that your way is often a better, smarter, happier one. Before you know it, you're the success you always wanted to be. And all you had to do was undertake an insanely pleasurable sex practice.

DOMINANCE WITHOUT RELEASE

To win at life, men must exert dominance. Over projects. Over habits. Over circumstances. Over obstacles. Over competition. Over failure. Without a dominant mindset, a man cannot succeed. Many men aren't comfortable with dominance. They're afraid to unleash their true power. But dominance is just another word for success.

Sex is the perfect success mindset training. Against all obstacles and odds, here I am lovingly connecting with this woman. Sex hypnotizes men to believe: I am a success. I dominate. I am the man. The more sex you have, the more you start to believe it.

Unfortunately 99.9% of men make one fatal mistake that kills the benefit of sexual dominance mindset training. They cum.

Some call it a *release*... and it is. Orgasm *releases* all your built-up energy and potential. Of course, orgasm also triggers a neurochemical feel-good jackpot. Orgasm evolved as the master reward for reproductive attempts. But most men gift themselves this ultimate prize every day - just for being such a great guy.

Not the Karezza gentleman - he has cracked the code. The Karezza gentleman doesn't want release. He keeps his neurochemistry on a slow steady drip, drip, drip. When he accomplishes something huge he'll get a spike, and then the next time he'll be forced to accomplish something even bigger to achieve that same rush. This is how to use dopamine tolerance to your advantage.

Karezza sex is the ultimate dominance mindset training because it separates the hypnosis-like benefits of sex from the drawbacks of release and immediate gratification. The Karezza gentleman trains nightly, channeling his masculine energy into pure, loving, gentle, respectful dominance without release.

Instead of letting off steam, the Karezza gentleman purifies his steam in bed, then uses it to power his transmutation engine. Great success requires sustaining a dominant mindset coupled with the ability to delay gratification indefinitely. Very few men today can manifest this mindset. Now you know exactly how to cultivate it: Karezza sex.

KAREZZA SEX: THE CURE FOR EVERYTHING

Lack of confidence. Procrastination. Anxiety. Depression. Inability to focus. Low energy. Suppressed masculinity. These issues plague men today. If only there were a cure. If only that cure was as ridiculously simple as getting naked with a woman and making out for hours with your penis inside her, whispering sweet, loving affirmations to each other. Too good to be true? Not at all. This is harmony with nature.

Cumming is for making babies. Sex without cumming is to build yourself into the man you want to be and create the life you want to live. Karezza sex fills you up on every level with pure, clean sexual energy that you can channel toward whatever noble purpose you choose. It's great for your woman too.

Karezza sex is nothing short of life-changing and it doesn't take long to reap the benefits. Your health will improve, your relationship will improve, your income will improve, your productivity will improve, your creativity will improve, your mood will improve, your focus and concentration will improve.

Everything in your life will improve with Karezza sex. Nothing will get worse. Who wouldn't trade two seconds of pleasure a few times a week for all that? And those are just the benefits to you personally. Karezza sex also has the potential to change the world.

THE WORLD TODAY

If you could sum up the prevailing mood today it would probably be: anxiety. People have lost touch with nature and love and everything that matters. They're anxious and can't figure out why. So they fight the anxiety itself. With pills, with porn, with virtual reality, with social media, with overeating, with booze, with passive pursuits.

The anxiety never goes away, of course. It only gets worse. As do the habits indulged in to cover it up. It's a vicious cycle that ends in death at the end of an unfulfilling life. A missed opportunity to take advantage of everything this phenomenal world has to offer.

We live in a time of unparalleled opportunity, access to valuable information, tools to make a living, and ways to do whatever you can dream up. Yet, besides a small sliver of the population, people are becoming more passive and helpless than ever. Something is wrong.

SEXUAL SOLDIERS

What if the whole world practiced Karezza sex? Can you imagine how happy everyone would be? How smoothly things would run? It seems unlikely in our current culture, but things can change. In ancient times, nobody even dreamed of today's technology and lifestyle. But step by step we got here.

It will take a whole generation of trailblazers for Karezza sex to become mainstream and have a societal impact. In the meantime, we early adopters are in the enviable position of having all the benefits to ourselves.

Imagine a secret hack that makes you a million times better and more effective in every way. This hack is free to everyone, and insanely pleasurable to boot. Now imagine only .01% of men take advantage of it. This small handful of men will surely dominate. Almost effortlessly.

The Karezza gentleman leads the way. He doesn't give a shit what everyone else does. He thinks for himself. He swims upstream. He loves women. He wants to lead one lucky girl on the most rewarding journey of her life - an adventure she won't find anywhere else that gives her the chance to blossom and achieve her potential.

The Karezza gentleman is a sexual soldier for a better world. Find a woman (if you don't have one) and teach her Karezza sex. Do it every night. Create positive energy flow. Then go out into the world and do positive things. Become the most audacious version of yourself imaginable. Create big ripples that alter the trajectory of this world. What are you waiting for?

A VISION OF THE FUTURE

"As future generations understand the law of spiritual growth and mastery their children will be superior in power and achievement to any heretofore known." - **Dr. Alice B. Stockham, *Karezza, Ethics of Marriage***

The year is 2070. Karezza sex has become widespread on Earth and is also practiced in deep space colonies and on Mars. Spacecraft powered by kinetic energy from Karezza sex shuttle people around the solar system with zero carbon emissions.

Wednesdays everyone works a half day then enjoys a 3 hour Karezza sex session with their partner. If you're single you can attend a Karezza networking event to meet potential partners. Cities are full of Karezza hotels where couples can go for a few hours during the day or evening at a reasonable rate to enjoy quiet, distraction-free Karezza sex. This is done openly and proudly, not in secret.

In the summer, healthy radiant people from all walks of life gather at sexual energy festivals where hundreds of Karezza couples - scattered a respectable distance apart for privacy - all have Karezza sex at the same time outdoors in the fresh air, in the sunshine, generating a massive swell of pure positive sexual energy that resonates deeply with the participants and the surrounding land, creating sexual energy supernovas.

In the year 2070, Karezza sex is taught in schools and advocated by medical professionals as the secret to health, happiness, and longevity. Karezza sex has become the normal, default way to have sex. The vast majority of babies are now conceived during loving, connected intercourse by stable couples with long-standing Karezza relationships.

In 2070, people are treating each other with a newfound respect and tenderness. People are getting in better touch with their bodies, minds, emotions, and spirits. The population is healthy, productive, and thriving. Masculinity and femininity are both widely recognized and appreciated as forces of good to be cultivated and proudly utilized.

In 2070, *The Gentleman's Guide To Karezza Sex* is inducted into the Intergalactic Library of Congress as an Important Historical Work. Men and women once again enjoy the slow dance of dating and getting to know each other. People are back in touch with the joys of transmuting sexual energy.

In 2070, there are less suicides, less rapes, less murders, less overdoses, less obesity, less divorce, less pornography, less masturbation, less cheating, less despair, less depression, less anxiety, less hopelessness, less misery.

In 2070, there's more love, more sex, more stable relationships, more honesty, more caring, more masculine men, more feminine women, more smiles, more enthusiasm, more adventure, more epiphanies, more strokes of genius, more optimism, more confidence, more risk-taking, and more joy.

Does all this seem unlikely? If you've read and absorbed the wisdom in this book, it shouldn't seem so far-fetched. All it takes is an elite generation of sexual soldiers to take up this practice and set the example.

Ultimately, what we do every day matters. This is especially true when it comes to sex, which is the primal source of our energy, drive, and passion. Practicing Karezza sex isn't only about building a better life for yourself and your woman. It's about building a better world for future generations. And that's a very gentlemanly thing to do.

CHAPTER 14:
NEXT STEPS AND PRO TIPS

CONGRATULATIONS

Congratulations! By completing this book you've taken a giant leap forward in your life. And this is no ordinary leap, because the end of this book is your gateway to the most rewarding journey imaginable.

From here, the rest is up to you. If you read this book carefully and apply its techniques and solutions you'll do great. Here are a few Pro Tips to guide you on your way.

PRO TIP #1 : TRACK YOUR PROGRESS

Competition is a huge motivator for men. This is by design to move our species forward. Use that to your advantage. Track your progress on orgasm retention and compete with yourself. There may be slip-ups along the way. If you accidentally orgasm, always try for a longer streak the next time around.

Keep track of your Karezza sex numbers too. Record exactly how many times each day, week, month, year you're doing it and try to keep pushing that number upward. This will get you in better shape, make you happier, and force you to manage your time better. It will also improve your relationship - because if that's not going smoothly you won't be setting any new sex records.

PRO TIP #2: SPREAD THE WORD

Once you've mastered the basics and start getting results, you can selectively let other high quality men in on your secret, whether online or in real life.

Before long people in your orbit will start asking you what's changed - what are you doing differently? Tell them. Give a friend or male relative a copy of this book if you think he could benefit from it - and who couldn't?

This isn't an entirely selfless gesture, either. We live in an orgasm world, so having a comrade or two in the same boat helps strengthen your own retention mindset.

Reviewing this book online is another powerful way to get the word out. You never know who might be inspired by your opinion.

PRO TIP #3: DON'T PANIC IF YOU DON'T HAVE A PARTNER

Karezza sex requires a woman, of course. If you don't have one yet, don't panic. Start (or continue) practicing orgasm retention and transmutation solo. Mastering that now will multiply your Karezza sex results later.

Use your time wisely. Pursue your purpose and become a leader in it. Sharpen your masculine polarity. Become a man who knows he has something to offer women.

Build yourself up and the women will flock to you or at least conveniently find themselves in your orbit. Good women need good men. Become one now and you'll never have to worry about women.

PRO TIP #4: KEEP THIS BOOK HANDY

As you make progress in the bedroom, you should re-read this book every once in a while to further sharpen your insight and master your art. This book is densely packed with tips, strategies, tactics, and solutions, so revisiting it as you progress through the ranks will prove beneficial.

PRO TIP #5: FURTHER READING

The Gentleman's Guide To Karezza Sex has been meticulously crafted to give you all the tools and knowledge you need to embark on the Karezza lifestyle successfully. Wisdom enough to fill entire libraries has been distilled down into the slim volume you just finished reading. The books below are also worth checking out if you want to deepen your knowledge and understanding of sexual energy, sexual transmutation, and Karezza sex.

The Karezza Method, or Magnetation: The Art of Connubial Love (1931 by J. William Lloyd

Written nearly a century ago, Lloyd's insights into masculinity, femininity, sex, and orgasm come across as surprisingly relevant and fresh today. Recommended for anyone who wants to dive deeper into the male/female dynamic with a spiritual twist.

Think and Grow Rich (1937) by Napoleon Hill

The great-granddaddy of all personal development and law of attraction programs, this book includes a thoughtful examination of sexual transmutation. Recommended for any man who wants to level up in life.

Cupid's Poisoned Arrow: From Habit to Harmony in Sexual Relationships (2009) by Marnia Robinson

Detailed and methodological in her approach, Robinson examines the science of orgasm and presents a first-person account of her own Karezza sex journey. This influential classic is recommended for anyone looking to dive deeper into the neurology of orgasm retention.

Karezza: Ethics of Marriage (1896) by Alice B. Stockham

Written by the doctor who coined the term "Karezza," this pioneering work of American sexology was revolutionary in its day and still feels relevant today. Recommended for anyone who wants to thoroughly master Karezza sex.

The Art of the Bedchamber (1992) by Douglas Wile

An indispensable sourcebook of ancient Chinese sex wisdom, Wile hunts down and translates the lost Chinese Sexual Yoga Classics dating back thousands of years. Recommended for anyone who wants to learn more about the Su Nu Ching and ancient Chinese sexology.

The Tao of Sexology (1986) by Stephen Chang

Chang's brand of Taoist sexology isn't always consistent with the goals of Karezza sex, but this illustrated volume offers an enlightening exploration of Taoist sex practices. Recommended for anyone looking to dive deeper into the Taoist perspective on sexual energy.

EPILOGUE:
WHY I WROTE THIS BOOK

I WROTE THIS BOOK TO CHANGE YOUR LIFE

There's a version of you that's happier, more alive, more socially free, more successful, more sexually satisfied, more in love, seizing every opportunity and making the most of it. Karezza sex is the most direct and powerful route to that better you.

Karezza sex combines the unrivaled power of sexual transmutation with the unparalleled benefits of a deeply connected intimate relationship. Karezza sex is the next-level, supercharged life hack that currently empowers an elite few but deserves to be discovered by worthy men everywhere. The technology to achieve unlimited success and happiness is now in your hands.

Men who begin this practice today have a huge competitive advantage over those who wait until everyone else is doing it. Don't wait, do it now.

I WROTE THIS BOOK TO MOVE HUMANITY FORWARD

Humanity has a lot to be proud of. But we're operating at only a small fraction of our potential. In many ways, we're stagnating and regressing. I wrote this book to help turn the tide and reset the course of humanity in a more positive direction.

Karezza sex has changed my life profoundly. A few years ago, I could barely manage to get by, let alone get ahead. Saving the world never would have occurred to me. Moving humanity forward just didn't seem like it was in the cards. Today it just seems like the natural thing to do.

Karezza sex changes your entire outlook on life. What didn't seem even remotely possible before, suddenly seems inevitable. The sexual energy you generate and retain has nowhere to go but up, and you will rise right along with it. A previous version of me barely had the energy to get through a busy day. Now I have so much energy I decided to spark a revolution.

Over the years, I've mastered every life hack you can imagine, from the law of attraction to hypnosis to underground knowledge and clandestine techniques. But nothing ever altered my life as positively and profoundly as Karezza sex. Once I witnessed this, I had no choice. I had to pay it forward.

In my coaching work, I guide men to transform their lives. One of the most common things I hear from my clients is "I never would have believed a year ago, I'd be where I am today." No matter how many times I hear this, it's always gratifying. This book is a chance to affect that type of real and permanent positive change on a massive scale.

I WROTE THIS BOOK TO SPARK A REVOLUTION

Once Karezza sex catches on with even a fraction of the population, imagine the genius, the accomplishment, the love, and the clean energy that will be unleashed into the world. But in order for Karezza sex to gain traction, an elite class of sexual soldiers must rise up, try it, practice it, and spread the word.

In his 1931 classic *The Karezza Method,* J. William Lloyd predicted that women, who felt sexually disempowered in that era, would rise up and spark a Karezza sex revolution to solve their problems. While women have been prominent in the Karezza movement, the mass uprising Lloyd envisioned never transpired.

Now it's men who are turning to Karezza sex to take our sexual power back. Gradually, men are waking up to the reality that the number one thing holding them back in life is frequent ejaculation and orgasm.

But the solution is not to walk away from women. Nothing could be less healthy than that. We must walk toward women, into their arms, and ultimately into their beds. But we must have a strategy and a gameplan. This book is that strategy. Karezza sex is that gameplan. The revolution is now.

-Nick Brothermore

www.brothermore.com

Made in the USA
Monee, IL
26 December 2024

75480857R00125